AIR WORDS

AIR WORDS

Writing Broadcast News in the Internet Age

John Hewitt

San Francisco State University

Fourth Edition

New York   Oxford

OXFORD UNIVERSITY PRESS

Oxford University Press, Inc., publishes works that further Oxford University's
objective of excellence in research, scholarship, and education.

Oxford   New York
Auckland   Cape Town   Dar es Salaam   Hong Kong   Karachi
Kuala Lumpur   Madrid   Melbourne   Mexico City   Nairobi
New Delhi   Shanghai   Taipei   Toronto

With offices in
Argentina   Austria   Brazil   Chile   Czech Republic   France   Greece
Guatemala   Hungary   Italy   Japan   Poland   Portugal   Singapore
South Korea   Switzerland   Thailand   Turkey   Ukraine   Vietnam

For titles covered by Section 112 of the US Higher Education Opportunity
Act, please visit www.oup.com/us/he for the latest information about
pricing and alternate formats.

Published by Oxford University Press, Inc.
198 Madison Avenue, New York, New York 10016
http://www.oup.com

Oxford is a registered trademark of Oxford University Press

Library of Congress Cataloging-in-Publication Data

Hewitt, John, 1943-
  Air words : writing broadcast news in the Internet age / John Hewitt.
    p. cm.
  ISBN 978-0-19-976003-9 (main text, pbk. : alk. paper)—ISBN 978-0-19-976004-6 (instructor's edition,
pbk. : alk. paper) 1. Television broadcasting of news. 2. Broadcast journalism—Authorship. I. Title.
  PN4784.T4H48 2011
  808.06607—dc22   2011006683

Printing number: 9 8 7 6 5 4 3 2 1

Printed in the United States of America
on acid-free paper.

BRIEF CONTENTS

CONTENTS

PREFACE

The last edition of *Air Words* was published a decade ago. Since that time, there have been wholesale changes in the journalism world. Print and broadcast journalism have downsized and the audience has embraced newer formats in online media. The Internet has blossomed with bloggers, aggregators, Really Simple Syndication (RSS) feeds, and social media sites. As we approach the year 2020, it's anyone's guess where this trajectory is headed.

It used to be that a journalist with a specialized skill—reporter, editor, photographer, television correspondent—could settle into a career. Now, anyone wanting to be a reporter or editor knows that proficiency in only one medium is a recipe for unemployment and they are best off with skills as multimedia practitioners.

But even with the expertise, multimedia-trained journalists are a bit adrift in how to pitch their talents to news agencies. Are they mass media reporters, convergence or multimedia journalists, bloggers, freelancers or V-Js? I heard of one reporter who referred to himself as an "open platform" journalist.

New to the 4th Edition

The journalism landscape is changing at meteoric speed and this demands a dramatic response for any textbooks used in the classroom. *Air Words* 4th Edition has surveyed instructors and students about their updated curricular needs and is packed with many significant revisions.

This newest edition of *Air Words* cannot escape the emerging legion of citizen journalists and the power of social media as newsgathering tools and communication channels. Chapters have been reorganized to

- survey the integration of online, smart phone, e-tablet and social media for presentation;

- explore social media's important ethical and legal quandaries;

- and to introduce comprehensive producing strategies that consider broadcast, online, and mobile devices.

Because traditional journalistic job roles are now ill-defined and in flux, the newest edition of *Air Words*

- outlines comprehensive skills needed by the Enterprise Journalist, the all-around news worker with powerful skills in story research, writing for spoken news, multi-media producing and visual storytelling;

- adds a chapter that concentrates on visual sequences and their logic;

- and enlarges the chapters on producing packages and writing tracks.

Finally, because instructors reinforced their confidence in the mastery learning concepts followed by this workbook, *Air Words* 4th Edition has

- added new graphics to strengthen its emphasis on workbook mastery learning and methodology;

- focused 10 new exercises on recent major news events;

- and expanded selected exercises for in-class group solutions.

Hope you enjoy.

Acknowledgments

Collaboration has always been a part of journalism. It is impossible to finish any single story or produce any newscast without the thoughtful assistance of colleagues who are reporters, producers, and editors. My years in journalism have brought me into contact with a marvelous cadre of professionals truly diligent about first-class news work. The on-the-job training of my first newspaper boss, Kenneth Leake of the Woodland *Daily Democrat,* and the thoughtful feedback from television news directors Tom Capra, Ron Miers, and Fred Zehnder polished my reporting skills.

Three decades of university teaching brought me into contact with wonderful journalist-teachers. Buzz Anderson, Bill Wenty, Stuart Hyde, and Marty Gonzalez of San Francisco State University; Fred Friendly of Columbia University; and Melba Beals of Dominican University taught me that any successful course must have solid teaching tools, including a structured workbook.

Feedback is essential to refine any book on writing. Many reviewers poured over earlier editions of *Air Words* and suggested important changes. My thanks to reviewers: Pam Tran, University of Alabama; David Moncreif, University of Tulsa; Elizabeth Emmert, Kutztown University; David Chanatry, Utica College; Jim LeTourneau, Western Kentucky University; Mel Hanks, Fort Hays State University; Jim Seward, St. John Fisher College; John McGuire, Oklahoma State University; William Raffel, Buffalo State College; Anne Donohue, Boston University; and Paul Glover, Henderson State University.

When preparing the 4th edition of *Air Words,* social media expert Alison Victor scoured the Internet to keep pace with its exploding viral world. News managers Lisa White, Dan Rosenheim, and Angie Sheets of KPIX in San Francisco gave me an opportunity to develop cogent chapters on reporter packages.

I am grateful for the help I got from Oxford University Press editors Peter Labella, Josh Hawkins, Mark Haynes, John Challice, copyeditor Deanna Hegle, production editor David Bradley, and staffer Caitlin Kaufman.

Finally, my wife and partner Annette Blanchard graciously supported my disappearing act while preparing this manuscript.

Thanks to all for the help. This fourth edition of *Air Words* is a true collaboration.

John Hewitt

Understand What Your Audience Needs

Former NBC news president Reuven Frank described news as the timely story of change as seen by an observer for an audience. Each word in that definition is crucial for journalists. This chapter is about the "timely," "observer," and "audience." It covers the storytelling unique to spoken and video media and how this engages an audience through updates, field recordings, emotion, personal delivery, and para-social relationships.

It also examines the career path for the 21st-century journalist.

Glossary

ACTUALITY Audio or video field recordings of interviews or events. Portions may be used in broadcast news or online multimedia packages.

ENTERPRISE In journalism, the effort by a single reporter or photojournalist to research, report, shoot, and compose a story.

E-TABLETS Easily portable electronic tablets with interactive Internet capabilities.

FTP SITES File Transfer Protocol. Can be used to automatically search and transfer files that fall into a desired topic.

PODCAST A spoken story recorded and available for download.

PUSH or PULL Description of direction in a media transaction. Media agencies push information to viewers; viewers pull data from online sources.

SMART PHONES Mobile handsets with easy Internet capability and large viewing screens.

SOCIAL MEDIA Term describing Internet sites such as Facebook or Twitter that are user-generated interactive home pages.

SOUNDBITE A portion of an actuality recorded interview that is scheduled for use in a spoken or video news story. Also referred to as a "sound pop."

USER-GENERATED CONTENT Term describing Internet sites such as YouTube or Wikipedia that allow posting of original video or archival material.

Who Is Watching, Listening, or Logging On

In the past, distributing news was a top-down operation. It was all push from the journalists. Only major news companies had the ad revenues that could bankroll staff to research, tap into international feeds, and package the news for delivery in newspapers, on television, or radio and on major online sites. These news purveyors relied on a dedicated, seemingly passive audience who adjusted their schedules to wait for the evening news. All of this was acomplished with little or no feedback.

But in the new century, significant advertising revenues followed the audience's passion for Internet sites. The newer users tracked information on their smart phones and e-tablets, listened to podcasts, and scoured home pages on laptops. They forwarded news via e-mail or social media and posted their own items or videos on user-generated sites like YouTube. They set up FTP sites where new online companies identified sources to alert them to specialized topics. And whereas traditional news staffs still originated

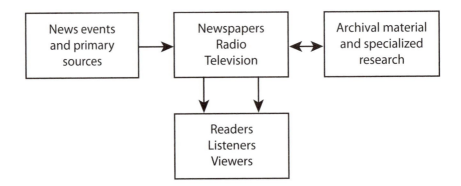

Figure 1.1 The earlier model. The mass media outlets covered the stories and did the research before delivering polished reports at their convenience to an audience measured in blocs. The audience had little access to original sources or alternative reports. Advertising paid for this system. Career journalists assumed the sales departments would provide the revenue for a life's work.

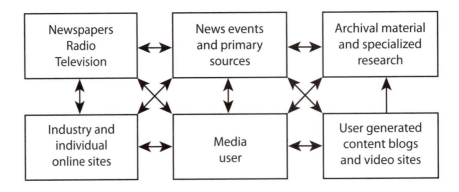

Figure 1.2 The post 2010 model. It is a transactional push-pull system in which the news event is the center and the audience suddenly becomes an empowered user. Revenue from advertising is fragmented. A career in journalism, based on a long-term media business plan, is chancy. Post-2010 journalists must be multiskilled opportunists ready to work for news agencies that cross media.

stories, their repostings on other sites were now attracting the all important ad dollars (see Figures 1.1 and 1.2).

Despite the ambiguities and fear about the future of news companies, each medium still retained its inherent characteristic strengths and weaknesses.

What Audience Research Tells Us About Media Strengths

The general public consistently tells survey takers that radio, television, and the Internet are important sources of news. The audience listens to radio, watches television, or logs onto the Internet for the latest and most immediate information. They pay attention to actualities on radio or watch videos on televison or Internet because these original sources can deliver an eyewitness and emotional impact. They read newspapers for local news and turn to television or Internet blogs because they trust in the personal delivery of information.

Fledgling reporters and writers should understand the audience's divided attention. Listeners and viewers and online users are multitasking while attending to the news. Most of the radio audience and more than half of the television audience are doing something else while these newscasts are on the air including cooking, eating dinner, taking care of children, lying in bed, multitasking online, texting friends, or even reading books.

For the Internet, research by Visible Measures, a company that consults for online video, reported in 2010 that one-fifth of the audience abandons Internet videos after :10 (ten seconds) and 45 percent are gone after a minute. Although this study of viewer abandonment concerned commercially produced videos, it is significant for any news stories added to a Web site. Consider too that laptop or smart phone users might be in nosiy, crowded coffee shops or airports where multiple distractions compete with your news stories. With audience attention drifting in and out, it takes clever leads and a sharply defined style to bring them into each and every story.

In broadcast, the audience gets one and only one chance to hear the story. Research has sorted out what the viewer or listener perceives, retains, and understands from the newscast. Stories written in direct speech patterns, with the least complex phrasing, are the easiest to digest in that crucial single pass. News writers must work to develop a simple style that promotes maximum understanding. If using video, writers also have to be aware that powerful visuals distract viewers and lessen comprehension.

Traditional News Values Offer Cues to Effective News Presentation

On a good news day, you might have three or four major stories. Some will be interesting and attract viewers no matter how you source or organize the story. You'll have to botch these to keep people from watching.

On a slow news day, there may not be any major stories; in fact, you may have to get all you can out of medium-interest stories, second-tier follow-ups, or features. For those, you might look for the interesting angle among these traditional categories:

- *Effect on the viewers.* People are very interested if their money, jobs, personal security, or family are threatened. This is known by some as "heart, health, and pocketbook."

- *Proximity.* Viewers and listeners gravitate to stories that involve people or events close to them, in their neighborhood, their city, and other nearby regions.

- *Prominence.* Prominence is based in stories about highly visible personalities such as entertainment stars, religious leaders, or politicians. Also, it involves any stories about national or international governmental actions at a high level; actions in the area of social order such as war; or social events or themes that carry an importance solely by definition such as health, education, or science.

- *Human Interest.* People enjoy stories about successes, failures, and curious events of unknown people as well as stories about common, everyday happenings in life.

Spoken News Strengths

Print journalism always had advantages; it was the original push-pull media. Newspapers could be read at any time, were portable, pushed massive amounts of news, had specialized sections—and best of all allowed the readers to scan the pages and pull what they wanted. There is no question that journalism flourished with this much reader involvement.

Online news sites offer the same opportunities. The user can set out in many directions seeking stories, including accessing the primary source material formerly only available to news departments.

But spoken news or video news has its strengths—immediacy, actuality, emotion, and personal delivery.

Immediacy

News is a collection of timely summaries of current events. In major news stories, after the initial alert arrives in almost any form, audiences turn to radio or television for the latest update, comprehensive coverage, or the last review of the evening.

This dictates a constant search for the update, the new information or angle that advances the story. Fresh leads must be prepared quickly. To get this immediacy, news staffs may never leave the office and instead do reporting and interviews on the phone or by interactive video on Internet sites such as Skype. Television needs the pictures and spends huge sums on microwaves, uplink trucks, and satellites designed to connect any location with their studio.

This pursuit of immediacy can be a drawback. Television, radio, and online staffs work under crushing deadlines that shorten the time needed to evaluate sources and review information. Reporters on site doing live shots often have arrived only moments before at the location. There is little time to thoroughly doublecheck facts, so rumors slip into reports.

Actuality

This carries the visceral and emotional impact. These recorded video and audio segments give the audience a sense of being on the scene. Radio has the rich natural sound of voices or happenings; television and online add the visual dimension. Audiences tell polltakers that one reason they turn to video is they like to see and hear people in the news so they can judge for themselves whether a person is telling the truth.

Emotion

The emotional content in video or image stories is powerful. It surpasses print-based accounts that concentrate on rational cause and effect or lists of details. Broadcast actualities, soundbites, and visuals have restored emotion to an important place in stories.

Emotion, however, is tricky and must be kept in proper perspective. When pictures and actualities with strong emotion become a story's driving force, it rightfully verges on sensationalism. The emotional content blows out the deeper meaning. Emotion should be treated with great care.

Personal Delivery and the Para-Social Relationship

Exactly how an on-air or online personality relates to the audience is vital to both credibility and sustaining an audience. Researchers have termed this the para-social or cyberlike relationship.

Certain non-news factors can enhance this relationship. A successful newscaster needs credibility, a well-written script, and an intriguing or comfortable personality to communicate the item in an effective manner.

The writer must consider his or her role in bolstering this relationship. When the newscaster reads a story, it is as if the writer is speaking. And if you are that writer, you must take great pains to achieve conversational sytle. This means smoothing the sentence flow, checking the accuracy of the story, and preparing the actualities and visuals. The era of simply reading what was written for print has long since passed. Awkward, print-style writing in a broadcast script will make your on-air reporters sound clumsy.

In the past, broadcast newsrooms were cut off from the community. The audience knew little about what went on inside a broadcast station and had almost no chance for feedback. Stations had to spend a fortune on promotion and relied on community appearances to personalize the presenters.

This isolation has changed in the ear of online blogs, chats, and social media gaints like Facebook and Twitter. Whereas some staffs have madatory blog and Twitter duties, others leave it up to the individual. Sheri Nelson of KFOG radio says social media are "closest" to her audience and foster the audience's sense of getting behind the scenes at the radio station. The audience is encouraged to join in the news process, especially in the area of sending in tips to stories.

Online Strengths

These media carry the same strengths as broadcast but with the addition of offering extensive primary sources, comprehensive coverage, inexpensive access, a vague legal world, and a feedback loop. And there may be powerful considerations as yet uncovered.

Primary Sources

These can be provided at a news Web site with simple links or by dedicating a separate page for that particular data. It reassures the user that you have fashioned your report on a credible basis.

The drawback can be a confusing home page layout for the user. Setting out too many choices makes finding your polished reports a chaotic quest. Web site design must be considered.

Comprehensive Coverage

The comprehensive nature of the Web page offerings allows reporters an opportunity to link the audience to a multitude of backgrounders or older features. Again, the danger here is overloading the Web site with material that distracts from your best current stories, either in print display or in audio/video.

Inexpensive Access

Getting the Web site up and on servers is easy, and a small, experienced crew can maintain it. There is no need for a building or extensive staff. You can also share newsgathering with other news agencies. The danger with this strength is the crowded field and competition from other sites.

Vague Legal World

A dubious online strength is the questionable legal status for information. Whereas traditional media are bound by clearly defined legal restrictions of copyright, libel, slander, and invasion of privacy, the fuzzy legalities of online research and presentation makes it easier to attempt difficult stories. The question of whether or not bloggers qualify for protection under shield laws is complex, and a New Jersey judge recently found against a blogger. Until the courts lock down the responsibility issues, this confusion leaves a gray area for the reporters and editors.

Feedback Loop

The Internet provides your audience with a comfortable avenue to approach the staff. Viewers can e-mail, post on their Facebook page, or even tweet to suggest that they are unhappy with the work you did on a story. Sometimes this aggressive feedback inflow needs attention, but it also strengthens your bonds with the audience. One news director said it was occasionally annoying but extremely valuable and had ordered each news producer to answer every e-mail query that is not a rant.

Different Strengths Lead to Different Approaches

Radio and television reporters often use different methods from those print reporters need to gather information about current events. When a news story is prepared, broadcast's strengths will often suggest a unique lead—a broadcast lead. On occasion, the lead might stress what's in the actualities or soundbites. Other times, it will be highlight the story's immediacy or the newscaster's ability in presentation. In any case, broadcast needs to choose its own angle for the story lead in accord with what's best for the medium and for the audience.

The Different Flow and Rhythm for Scripts for Spoken News

Broadcast or Web-presented spoken stories are designed to mimic conversational English. The scripts cannot take the approach that they are well-written print magazine articles that someone will read to the audience. Why should the audience sit through that? No they shouldn't: broadcast writing is a dialogue, with a sentence structure more analogous to a theater presentation. The broadcast phrasing must be shorter, more informal, and follow a storytelling narrative form. To facilitate more compact sentences, many news stylebooks discourage punctuation beyond the period, question mark, or comma and often replace that comma with three dots. See Figure 1.3 for examples.

Thirty thousand residents of the Southern California towns of Pasadena, La Canada and Glendale were forced to flee their homes by the threat of mudslides from recent nearby forest fires, according to CalFire emergency officials. The neighborhoods were at the base of a mountain left barren after a wildfire burned over 100,000 acres in the Angeles National Forest last August.	THE THREAT OF MUDSLIDES IN SOUTHERN CALIFORNIA IS FORCING MORE EVACUATIONS. SOME 30-THOUSAND RESIDENTS OF PASADENA . . . LA CANADA . . . AND GLENDALE HAVE FLED THEIR HOMES. THEIR NEIGHBORHOODS ARE DIRECTLY BELOW A MOUNTAINSIDE BURNED IN LAST AUGUST'S WILDFIRES. THOSE FIRES DESTROYED OVER 100-THOUSAND ACRES IN THE ANGELES NATIONAL FOREST.
Major indexes on the New York Stock Exchange fell almost three percent today on rumors of higher Department of Labor unemployment figures expected to be released tomorrow. Investors are still worried the economy is taking longer to recover from the three-year recession, according to stock analysts at several online trading sites.	STOCKS SHARPLY LOWER TODAY. THE MAJOR INDEXES FELL ALMOST THREE PERCENT. ANALYSTS THINK INVESTORS ARE WORRIED ABOUT NEW UNEMPLOYMENT FIGURES. THOSE JOBLESS TOTALS ARE EXPECTED TOMORROW.

Figure 1.3 Example of story text in print (left) and in broadcast (right).

The differences are both stylistic and structural. The broadcast narrative follows the rhythms of speech and is written for the ear. It uses shorter sentences while releasing facts in bursts.

In almost every exercise in this workbook, we'll be encouraging you to write to mimic speech patterns. Before you go on, you should complete Exercise 1A to see what your speech looks like.

▶ **EXERCISE 1-A**

What Your Speech Looks Like

For this exercise, you'll need a colleague and an audio recorder. The purpose is to produce a printed transcript of your normal speech patterns.

To begin, read the following story material several times. Then put down the book, and with the recorder on, relate your account conversationally as if you were sitting in a coffee shop and were telling a colleague about this story. Don't write a script or even notes for what you are going to say. Your storytelling is meant to be impromptu, even casual. This narrative should run :30 to :45 (forty-five seconds).

When you finish, type an exact transcription of what you said. Exact. Be truthful. The transcript should include every stumble, half-sentence, "uhmm," "awesome," "like," or whatever words you used describe what was going on.

Situation Notes

The location: A zoo in your city that we'll call the Leopard Creek Zoo.

The event: Two great pandas are expected amidst a flurry of civic activity. The mayor, the delegation from the nearby Chinese consulate, zookeepers, reporters, and television crews have gathered. A large delivery truck pulls up, and after several speeches, the pandas, in their special wooden packing cages, are lifted from a long flatbed trailer. The rare animals are on loan from the zoo in Bejing for two months, during which time they will be housed in a special climate-controlled building. The pandas' diet consists of blue bamboo shoots. It'll be two weeks before the public views them.

....

....

....

....

....

....

....

The Enterprise Journalist

In the past, major newspapers or broadcast stations had well-staffed assignment desk operations from which an editor would dispatch crews (reporters/photographers) to gather the stories. Back in the newsroom, support staff (photo editors/video editors) waited to process the material. But industry cutbacks have forced general assignment journalists in medium-sized or large cities to revert to what their brethren in smaller cities or bureaus had always done—shoulder more of the newsgathering process.

These days a reporter might be asked to be a jack-of-all-trades, the so-called one-man band. Reporters might be called on to take pictures, shoot video, edit the pictures, and prepare the final story directly for air or Web design for online. Whether a plus or minus for the news community, this short staffing is defining a new era in which reporters must also be enterprise journalists, working informal beats and always seeking stories to pitch for coverage while developing personal skills in the supplementary crafts.

Research Made Easier

Researching news stories used to be the exclusive arena of the journalist. At one time, only news staffs had access to primary printed sources, old clips, archival video, or an entrée to people with guarded information. But now blogs, social media, and YouTube have changed the equation. News users can access many of the same sources as journalists.

This is not to say that traditional journalistic research methods should be abandoned. Journalists should be cautious of single-source stories. It is significant that the Project for Excellence in Journalism at Columbia University used (1) Mulitple Sources and (2) Expertise of Sources as two of its checkpoints for assessing quality in news. There is a solid benefit of probing multiple primary sources. This is often the way to find a diversity of viewpoints, new story ideas, followup ideas, and confirm facts. In this millenium, no journalist worth his or her salt will ever succeed without at least mastering critical tools: the telephone, Internet search engines, and social media.

Phone Research for Local Information

Old-time news reporters had a rule: Never get off the phone until you have the information you called for. Talking to sources is still the best way to get local information.

- Get a headset if you are comfortable with that.

- Be prepared to write down information in readable notes.

- Using directories and the Internet, locate as many sources as you can.

Sources can be divided into two camps—primary and secondary. Primary sources are recognized experts, eyewitnesses, and persons directly affected by the story. You can ask these people tough questions and rely on the answers.

If they don't have strong credentials for expert testimony, if they are retelling the eyewitnesses' story they heard from someone else, if they knew of someone affected by the story, or if they are a blogger or news aggregator, then they qualify as secondary sources. You may need to verify their tips and facts through other sources.

Online Research

Two decades ago, computer investigations were a dream; but now, a journalist can't live without the Internet. Search engines, all-encompassing databases, bloggers, the partial privacy of social media, user-generated sites, primary documents, maps, and national phone directories are a gold mine for those who know how to use them. And keeping up on new Internet pathways is necessary; today's hot search engine may not exist tomorrow.

Aggregators. These are non-news agencies or individuals who survey certain news and corporate Web sites usually for stories focused on a single topic. After gathering material, RSS feeds can then redirect their findings to persons or reporters who have signed up.

Blog specialists. These are insider news gatherers who may work alone or with a staff to provide the latest breaking news to an audience. Some operations, such as the Huffington Post, are extensive and have solid reputations.

User-generated content. Sites such as YouTube, Vimeo, and social media offer free posting of video and/or photographs. This can be a dangerous area for producers hungry for visual story support. Copyrights and privacy concerns are paramount. Stations continually work on questions of access to these postings and whether they can be reposted on station Internet sites or used in broadcast stories.

Social media. Sites such as Facebook or Twitter allow news staffs to find unrecognized stories, sample the public interest in issues, and find examples of individuals who might be primary sources or directly affected by public policy. One news director said her staff used Facebook and Twitter as a way to reach out to the public when researching a breaking news story or a backgrounder on mortgage foreclosures. A quick posting and tweet found witnesses to a campus shooting and turned up a number of respondents who were families struggling with house payments.

Social media sites have been instrumental in getting citizen particpation in more involved investigatory efforts. A good example was the continuing British story about expense account abuse by members of Parliament. Although the *Daily Telegraph* first took on the story, *The Guardian* picked up the thread and by exhorting their readers to join in, managed to get 27,317 people to review over 200,000 documents. This led to a continuing investigation on an issue that began in 2009.

▶ **EXERCISE 1-B**

Looking for Archives

Using local internet resources as suggested by your instructor, find at least three recent comprehensive stories about these topics and bring copies to class.

1. The local crime rate.

2. A local environmental battle between developers and citizens.

3. The direction of local business activity. What sectors are up, down, improving, or declining.

4. Local housing prices. Up? Down?

....

....

....

▶ **EXERCISE 1-C**

General Searches

Using any available search engine and locate

1. A site to give us information about U.S. government Superfund toxic site cleanup.

2. A site with information on safety defects in light pickup trucks.

3. A group urging a stop to the proliferation of land mines in the world.

4. A site to explain the Consumer Price Index and what it reports.

....

....

....

► **EXERCISE 1-D**

Social Media Searches

Use any convenient social media site to probe background information on celebrities selected by the class.

....
....
....
....
....
....

► **EXERCISE 1-E**

Finding Government Sites

On a separate page, list

1. Three government sites that explore airliner saftey.

2. Three government sites that tell you about regional transportation planning.

3. Get the phone number and bios of two local congressional representatives.

....
....
....
....
....
....
....

► **EXERCISE 1-F**

Finding the Expert

For many stories, you will need to talk directly to a recognized authority. How do you find an expert? Use business directories to locate the firm that you want, and then using their Web sites, or simple phone calls, you can go from there.

Conduct a search to locate the name and phone number of an expert on

1. Auto braking systems.

2. Jail reform programs.

3. Elementary education programs

....
....
....
....
....
....
....
....

Chapter Summary

This chapter has covered the different strengths of broadcast and online media. Working journalists should understand that significant advantages are gained by writing in a format that works best for a particular medium. To work in the 21st century journalism field, reporters and researchers should also become confident in online research and evaluating the quality of those sources.

2

Making Some
Major Changes

We've all been taught to write for print. Teachers praised long sentences with careful intro and interior phrases, meaningful words, and lists of facts. That style is still useful in academia or, in some stylebooks, for newspapers.

The purpose of this workbook is to write for spoken news. Your audience only gets one chance to hear the information or see the video. For this reason, we encourage newswriting that is crisp, informal, and structured as conversation.

This chapter covers steps designed to shift your style from print to spoken news.

Glossary

ELLIPTICAL SENTENCE A sentence fragment designed to mimic speech patterns. It could be missing subjects or verbs.

NESTED PHRASE Mid-sentence phrase that breaks up the continuity of the sentence elements, usually the subject and verb.

PRONOUNCER The phonetic spelling of a word in a spoken story. Usually the pronouncer is broken into syllables and placed in the copy behind the true spelling of the word. For example, the Greek last name Pitarakis would have a pronouncer "(pea-dar-A-KEES)." The pronouncer is the writer's responsibility.

Seven Crucial Steps When Writing for the Ears (Broadcast) Versus Writing for the Eyes (Newspapers)

Our approach to writing for spoken news is based loosely on these considerations:

- A viewer will hear the story once and not be able to read it. Simplicity is the answer for that.

- An anchor or news presenter will have to have to read aloud the sentences or stories you write. For this reason, your scripts should strive to mimic dialogue or conversational speech. They must also have a pace that allows comfortable breathing.

To achieve this conversational style, we begin by exploring restrictions on

- Sentence or phrase length.

- Punctuation.

- Details and information exclusion.

- Careful language.

Start With Short Sentences

The changeover from prose to speech begins by thinking short. Long sentences work well in print. They are structured to let your eye dart back and forth across the sentence, reconnect the facts, evaluate the attribution, and tie the the causes to the effects.

Here's a print sentence from a newspaper source:

"Four San Jose homes were damaged early this morning, one seriously, in a series of apparent arson fires in the East San Jose area that may have all been set by the same suspects, Police Sgt. Ronnie Lopez of the San Jose Police Department said."

This sentence is difficult for broadcast. It is designed to tie together facts, and its length would force the speaker unnaturally to pause for breath. To convert that information for spoken news, we can easily break it into thirds, trying to keep our word count down for each segment:

THERE WERE APPARENT ARSON FIRES IN FOUR HOMES IN EAST SAN JOSE THIS MORNING. ONLY ONE HAD SERIOUS DAMAGE. POLICE SAID THE SAME SUSPECTS MAY BE RESPONSIBLE.

▶ **EXERCISE 2-A**

Breaking Up Print Sentences

Here are a few print sentences. Try breaking these tongue-twisters into two sentences, each fewer than fifteen words, or even three sentences:

"Montana's public school districts are spending too much annually to replace or repair hundreds of school roofs by employing a practice that restricts cost-saving competitive bidding and makes taxpayers pay up to double what they otherwise would spend, an investigation has found." (42 words)

....

....

....

....

....

"Web giant Google must stand trial in a lawsuit by a fired 54-year-old manager who said co-workers called him an 'old man' and a 'fuddy-duddy' while bosses told him he was a bad 'cultural fit' in the youth-oriented company, the state Supreme Court ruled Thursday." (45 words)

....

....

....

....

....

"Moscow was engulfed Wednesday by the thickest blanket of smog yet this summer, an acrid, choking haze from wildfires that have wiped out many nearby Russian forests and a military base that are now making the air over the Russian capital a health hazard." (44 words)

....

....

....

....

....

Eliminate Long Introductory Phrases

Our next objective is to avoid setting up a precondition in a long dependent introductory phrase or clause. Prose writers often use these long phrases to vary sentence structure; but, as a general rule, these phrases are to be avoided in broadcast. Any sentence with a long, complex opening phrase should be rewritten either as a compound sentence or as two separate ones.

Here is an example of a long introductory phrase:

ALTHOUGH THE TRANSIT DISTRICT REPAIRED THE LIGHT RAIL CARS AND HAD THEM BACK ON THE TRACKS LAST THURSDAY . . . NO ONE IS SAYING YET WHEN THE COMMUTE SCHEDULES WILL RETURN TO NORMAL.

Here's the rewrite:

THE TRANSIT DISTRICT REPAIRED THE LIGHT RAIL CARS AND HAD THEM BACK ON THE TRACKS LAST THURSDAY.
THERE IS STILL NO WORD ON WHEN COMMUTE SCHEDULES WILL RETURN TO NORMAL.

▶ **EXERCISE 2-B**

Working With Unneeded Intros

In each case, isolate the introductory phrase by making it into a second sentence.

ALTHOUGH THE ROADSIDE TESTS HAD ADDED STRENGTH TO THE NATIONAL CRACKDOWN ON DRUNK DRIVERS . . . THE SUPREME COURT HAS RULED STATES MUST REVISE THE RULES FOR SURPRISE SOBRIETY CHECKPOINTS.

....
....
....

ALTHOUGH FOREIGN POLICY WAS A MAJOR CAMPUS FLASHPOINT SEVERAL YEARS AGO . . . UNIVERSITY STUDENTS TODAY ARE MORE CONCERNED WITH PERSONAL CAREER ISSUES.

....
....
....

Very Short Intros Are Okay

An exception to this rule allows the use of short introductory (two- to four-word) phrases that convey information about time or place. Here are two short introductory phrases that add to the story:

> UNTIL YESTERDAY . . . THE LOCAL UTILITY COMPANIES COULD CHARGE WHATEVER THEY WANTED.

> AND ALSO IN THE SOUTH BAY . . . SCHOOL OFFICIALS TOOK THE WRAPS OFF A NEW CHARTER SCHOOL.

Misplaced Phrases Cause Confusion

Phrases that add information sometimes end up quite a distance from the noun they modify. The so-called dangling modifier can alter the meaning of the sentence. Here's an example of a misplaced phrase:

> RAPPER OSIS WILL RECEIVE AN AWARD FOR HUMANITARIAN WORK ON THE DAILY SHOW.

Where was the humanitarian work done? At Comedy Central? The best solution is to reorganize the sentence. Here it is:

> RAPPER OSIS WILL APPEAR ON THE DAILY SHOW TO RECEIVE AN AWARD FOR HUMANITARIAN WORK.

▶ **EXERCISE 2-C**

Misplaced Phrases

Rewrite these sentences that have misplaced phrases:

> THERE IS NEW HOPE FOR A CURE FOR HEART DISEASE . . . WHICH IS WHAT MANY RESEARCHERS HAVE WANTED.

....

....

> COMPANY OFFICIALS SAID THEY WERE UNSURE WHAT CAUSED THE POL- LUTED AIR FROM THE DIESEL TANKS THAT COULD BE SEEN HOVERING OVER THE REFINERY.

....

....

Nested Phrases

Another problem is the nested phrase, an interior modifier that tells us more about a noun but that usually the splits the subject from the verb. If it is only two words, you can probably get away with it. However, most are longer and require a rewrite. Here's an example:

> THE STORM . . . <u>WHICH UNTIL YESTERDAY WAS NOTHING MORE THAN A LIGHT DRIZZLE</u> . . . BROUGHT A HEAVY DOWNPOUR AND THUNDER TO THE KEYSTONE COUNTIES.

This interior phrase could be confusing for broadcast narrative. How do you fix it? One solution is to convert it into two sentences:

> UNTIL YESTERDAY . . . THE STORM PRODUCED ONLY A LIGHT DRIZZLE. NOW IT IS BRINGING HEAVY RAIN AND THUNDER TO THE KEYSTONE COUNTIES.

Here's another example:

> THE SENATE . . . WHICH WILL ADJOURN FOR A MONTH-LONG VACATION TOMORROW . . . WORKED LATE LAST NIGHT.

And to fix it:

> THE SENATE WORKED LATE LAST NIGHT. THEY WILL ADJOURN TOMORROW FOR A MONTH-LONG VACATION.

▶ **EXERCISE 2-D**

Nested Fixes

Eliminate the nested phrases from these sentences by dividing them into two sentences or forming them into a compound sentence:

THE GAS PUMPS . . . WHICH WERE ORIGINALLY IN THE MARINA PLANS ALONG WITH NEW PIERS AND WALKWAYS . . . WILL COST A MILLION DOLLARS.

....
....
....
....
....
....

TEN OF THE WHALES . . . ON A MIGRATION FROM THE ARCTIC OCEAN TO THE WARMER WATERS OFF BAJA CALIFORNIA . . . BEACHED THEMSELVES YESTERDAY.

....
....
....
....
....
....

Consider Elliptical Sentences

Because broadcast writers aim to mimic informal speech patterns, news copy at some stations may have elliptical sentences—sentence fragments with implied but unspoken words or phrases. This style is most useful for a backgrounder or feature story and not as useful for breaking news, tragedies, or crime news.

The practice is controversial. Many anchors aren't comfortable with it. Many station stylebooks forbid it or caution against it. However, when allowed, elliptical sentences help to keep the word count down and reinforce conversational patterns.

Here's an example:

THE PRESIDENT . . . IN WASHINGTON . . . TRYING TO RESTORE CREDIBILITY . . .

IT'S THAT TIME OF YEAR AGAIN . . . SPRING BREAK. POLICE IN DAYTONA BEACH . . . WELL . . . THEY'RE WORRIED.

The speech pattern and delivery of a legendary radio news reporter is the classic example. One of his stories might go something like this:

IN NEW JERSEY. A TRAGEDY. A MAN . . . DESPONDENT . . . SUICIDE ON HIS MIND. BOUGHT A GUN. PUT THE BARREL TO HIS HEAD. PULLED THE TRIGGER.
DIDN'T WORK. BULLET MISSED. HIT THE WATER HEATER. IT BLEW UP AND BURNED THE MAN'S HOUSE DOWN.

If your station or news anchor doesn't object, it doesn't hurt to fashion the occasional elliptical sentence to give a conversational feeling to the writing.

Here's another example:

YES . . . IT'S ONLY LATE AUGUST.
BUT FORECASTERS HAVE A WARNING . . .
EARLY WINTER THEY SAY.
BELOW FREEZING TEMPERATURES ARE COMING.
AND THAT SHOULD EMBARRASS CITY OFFICIALS.
GREAT FALLS HASN'T OPENED UP THE SHELTERS YET.
HOMELESS ACTIVISTS SAY IMMEDIATE ACTION IS NEEDED.

► **EXERCISE 2-E**

Eliminating Words and Phrases

Examine this story for elliptical possibilities. Revise it by removing phrases or rewriting.

OAKLAND POLICE ARE NOW USING SMALL VIDEO CAMERAS TO RECORD ANY ENCOUNTER WITH CITIZENS.

THE TINY CAMERAS ARE THE SIZE OF CELLPHONES AND ARE WORN ON THE UNIFORM.

THE OFFICER CAN CHOOSE WHEN TO TURN ON THE CAMERA . . . BUT CANNOT ALTER OR ERASE THE RECORDINGS.

POLICE CAN USE THE FOOTAGE WHEN WRITING REPORTS.

....

....

....

....

....

....

....

....

....

....

....

....

Punctuation and Uppercase Style

Punctuation is usually restricted by the stylebook of individual stations. A general rule would be to use only the comma, the period, and the question mark. Forget about quotation marks, semicolons, colons, and "exclamation points." Do not <u>underline</u>, which in broadcast means to add vocal emphasis; instead, leave that to producers and newscasters for later use.

Some stations eliminate commas and replace them with three dots (. . .). Stations differ on whether to write copy in uppercase or lowercase letters.

In this workbook, we use three dots in place of the comma and write all scripts in upper case.

Learning to Exclude Story Elements

In print, there is often enough space to include every detail you can find. But in broadcast and online, a lack of time and/or space severely restricts what you can incorporate. So you must perfect the art of exclusion.

To shorten stories, consider the listener's or viewer's needs. There is no definitive research that tells us how many facts a viewer can remember; however, it is common sense that a few facts presented in the least complex sentences have the best chance of staying with the audience.

When you approach a story, review the information and decide what must get into the story. You are looking for the most significant fact or facts. Here's a list of items we exclude:

- Middle Initials. Unless the individual demands that they be included or there is a historical reason to include the initial, such as with former President George W. Bush, to distinguish him from his father, we skip them.

- Ages. In most cases, these are unimportant. Obviously, if a 97-year-old man robs a store, you've got a different angle to the story. But if the robber was 34 years old, then there is nothing unique in that.

- Addresses. Newspapers routinely put these in; broadcasters routinely ignore them.

- Unnecessary geographical data. Don't bore your audience with unnecessary streets and districts. Evaluate whether it is useful to say the story happened in the Inner Sunset District.

- Unnecessary attribution. Decide whether it's necessary to give the source's name.

- Unnecessary full titles. Either eliminate or shorten most titles. An "Undersecretary for Middle Eastern and Indian Subcontinental Affairs" could become a "STATE DEPARTMENT OFFICIAL."

- Decimal places. Any figure with decimal places has little chance of being remembered. Count those out almost immediately unless they are vital to the story.

Rounding Off Numbers

Broadcast newswriters often face stories with large amounts of data—percentages, numbers, dollar amounts, etc. If your goal is to have the audience retain information after one reading of the story, then you should practice rounding off this data.

If your story includes the number $24,473,000.25 as a city budget figure, you can round it off to "ALMOST 25-MILLION-DOLLARS." It is close enough to give the audience an approximation of the amount. When appropriate, change a figure like 9.56% into "ALMOST TEN PERCENT" or "ONE TENTH."

Writing Out Those Numbers to Be Spoken

When writing numbers to be read, there are some helpful rules:

- Spell out numbers from 1 to 11. Spell out qualifiers (million/thousand/hundred).
  ONE-COW
  FOUR-THOUSAND-DAYS

- Except for dates (2010), never use four digits in one number. For example, 999 works but 1,999 must be rewritten as ONE-THOUSAND-999.

- Spell out any qualifying symbols that may be misread (such as $, %, etc.).
  46-THOUSAND-DOLLARS or 26-PERCENT or 13-DEGREES.

▶ **EXERCISE 2-F**

Becoming an Excluder

Here's an example of copy with too much detail and number problems. Underline areas that you might shorten or eliminate and discuss these in class. Look for numbers that may have to be rewritten to make them more readable.

NEXT WEEK'S CHINESE NEW YEAR'S PARADE IN SAN FRANCISCO WILL FEATURE FOR THE FIRST TIME THREE LIGHTED DRAGONS BORROWED FROM SAN FRANCISCO'S SISTER CITY IN CHINA—SHANGHAI. THE ORGANIZERS SAY THE DRAGONS . . . WHICH ARE 200-FEET LONG AND CARRIED BY 40 DANCERS . . . ARE THE MOST POPULAR FEATURE.

THE VICE PRESIDENT FOR PARADE OPERATIONS CAROLINE B. FOGLESON-CHAN SAYS THAT IN ADDITION TO THE DRAGONS, THERE WILL ALSO BE 15 BANDS, 12 DRILL TEAMS, AND 20 FLOATS. THE TOTAL NUMBER OF MARCHERS THIS YEAR IS UP 11.5% . . . THE FIFTH YEAR THE PARADE HAS GROWN.

FOGLESON-CHAN SAID THE 97-MINUTE PARADE WILL LEAVE THE MISSION STREET HOLDING CENTER AT 6 P-M AND THEN WIND ITS WAY UP DRUMM STREET TO MARKET STREET—THEN MARKET STREET TO GEARY STREET—THEN GEARY STREET TO KEARNY BEFORE FINISHING UP AT PORTSMOUTH SQUARE.

AT LEAST 100,000 SPECTATORS SHOULD LINE THE PARADE ROUTE, SAY THE ORGANIZERS. BUT THE POLICE SAY THEY EXPECT IT WILL ONLY BE ABOUT 50,000.

▶ EXERCISE 2-G

Rewrite and Round Off

Rewrite this story into shorter sentences using a broadcast style:

> ACCORDING TO A REPORT BY THE ARIZONA REAL ESTATE CONSORTIUM RELEASED THURSDAY . . . FLAGSTAFF AREA MEDIAN PRICES FOR ALL HOME SALES IN MAY TOPPED $402,120 FOR THE FIRST TIME IN NEARLY 23-MONTHS. STILL . . . SALES OF MORE AFFORDABLE HOMES AND FORECLOSURES CONTINUED TO FALL BY NEARLY 9.5%.

....

....

....

....

▶ EXERCISE 2-H

Rewrite and Round Off

Rewrite this story into shorter sentences using a broadcast style:

> THE ONE MONTH OLD $24,600,000 SEWAGE TREATMENT TERTIARY REFINEMENT FACILITY . . . WHICH IS LOCATED ON THE SHORELINE AT BREMEMERS COVE . . . IS SHUTTING DOWN NEXT WEEK FOR REPAIRS.
>
> SEWAGE ADMINISTRATOR B. MELFORD BLOSSOM SAYS THEY HAVE TO DO THIS BECAUSE 525 GALLONS OF UNPROCESSED AND UNTREATED WASTE EFFLUENT . . . WHICH STILL NEEDED PROCESSING . . . LEAKED INTO THE NEARBY SLOUGH DURING HEAVY RAINS.
>
> BLOSSOM BLAMED THE SPILL ON A DESIGN FLAW IN A SUBSURFACE EXPANSION PUMP. IT WILL TAKE A MONTH TO FIX. THE CONSTRUCTION COMPANY WILL PICK UP THE $2,125,000 TAB FOR THE REPAIRS.

....

....

....

....

Read It Aloud!!!!

Although broadcast newsrooms look like any other office areas, there is a subtle difference. Most reporters and writers appear to be talking to their computer screens. In most cases, they are finishing the most important step in broadcast writing—reading the final version aloud. This practice uncovers awkward phrasing and finds words that need special emphasis.

Once you determine which words could benefit from emphasis, you need to mark them. Computer news systems have special function keys to highlight words for the prompter, and many newscasters also add underlining and slashes to add emphasis or short arrows to indicate a change in voice pitch.

Here's are examples of unmarked and marked copy:

> A NEW SURVEY IS REPORTING HIGH SCHOOL STUDENTS WILL HAVE SEEN AT LEAST 20-THOUSAND MURDERS IN THE MOVIES AND ON TV BY THE TIME THEY ENTER COLLEGE.
> THE REPORT FROM THE KAUFMANN SCHOOL OF COMMUNICATIONS AT GARDEN STATE UNIVERSITY SAYS THE EXPOSURE TO THIS MANY VIOLENT ACTS COULD DAMAGE THEIR PERSONALITIES . . . AND DESENSITIZE THEM TO COMMON KINDNESS.

Now, the same example with the highlighted marks:

> A NEW SURVEY IS <u>REPORTING</u> HIGH SCHOOL STUDENTS WILL HAVE SEEN AT LEAST <u>20-THOUSAND</u> MURDERS IN THE MOVIES AND ON TV // BY THE TIME THEY ENTER COLLEGE.
> THE REPORT FROM THE KAUFMANN SCHOOL OF COMMUNICATIONS AT GARDEN STATE UNIVERSITY SAYS THIS <u>EXPOSURE</u> TO MANY VIOLENT ACTS COULD <u>DAMAGE</u> THEIR PERSONALITIES . . . AND <u>DESENSITIZE</u> THEM TO COMMON KINDNESS.

► **EXERCISE 2-1**

Adding Rehearsal Marks and Reading Aloud

Review this story, read it aloud, and put in rehearsal marks for words or phrases you think need added emphasis, pauses, or vocal shifts.

AN OREGON MAN IN A 45-FOOT SAILBOAT REACHED BOSTON HARBOR ON WEDNESDAY . . . BREAKING A 140-YEAR-OLD RECORD FOR THE VOYAGE FROM SAN FRANCISCO.

THE SOLO SAILOR . . . DALE CREST . . . ENDURED STORMY SEAS AND GALE FORCE WINDS ON THE EAST COAST BUT STILL FINISHED IN 69 DAYS . . . MORE THAN SEVEN DAYS FASTER THAN THE PREVIOUS RECORD.

CREST SAID HIS TRIP WAS EXHAUSTING AND DANGEROUS AND HE WASN'T GOING TO TRY . . . QUOTE . . . TO DO SOMETHING THAT STUPID AGAIN.

THE THREE-MASTED CLIPPER SHIP NORTHERN LIGHT HELD THE PREVIOUS RECORD. THAT SHIP MADE THE TRIP IN 76 DAYS . . . OVER ONE HUNDRED YEARS AGO.

Chapter Summary

Broadcast scripts require attention to standards and style. The spoken copy must be short, free of interconnected phrases, and clear on numbers and details. If the station stylebook allows it, newswriters might pepare scripts in a shortened elliptical style. Reading the story aloud and adding emphasis markings is a final check for smooth scripts.

3

A Closer Look at Grammar and Word Choice

This chapter covers several structural changes vital to convert prose to broadcast writing including the use of the concise verbs and adjectives, repetition, attribution, active and passive voice, multiple tenses, and common reference problems.

Glossary

ACTIVE VOICE Verb form in which the entity or person responsible for the action precedes the verb.

ATTRIBUTION A crucial phrase that reveals the source of your information for a news story. Attribution helps establish credibility.

PASSIVE VOICE Verb form in which the thing or person responsible for the action follows the verb.

READER The most frequently used broadcast format. It is a story—usually short and under 40 seconds—read by the newscaster without actualities or remote reports.

Use Concise Verbs and Adjectives

Literary prose allows the use of complex, obscure verbs and adjectives, but conversational writing demands simplicity. Often, this means skillfully selecting the most easily understood word to replace a more complicated synonym.

Wordy Verb Forms

Look for the most direct way to express action. Double-check your verb and infinitive choices to see whether a more straightforward verb or infinitive conveys the same idea and makes the sentence easier to digest and remember. Here are some examples:

THE PANEL VOTED <u>TO TERMINATE THE CONSTRUCTION</u> OF THE BRIDGE.

Instead, you could have written

THE PANEL VOTED <u>TO STOP BUILDING</u> THE BRIDGE.

Or consider this example:

B-P BANDED TOGETHER A SPECIALIZED TEAM TO FIGHT THE LEAKING WELL.

Instead, you could have written

B-P CREATED A SPECIALIZED TEAM TO FIGHT THE LEAKING WELL.

▶ **EXERCISE 3-A**

Simplify the Verbs

Rewrite to simplify the verbs in these sentences:

MEXICAN DRUG CARTELS HAVE COALESCED THEIR POSITION IN THAT COUNTRY'S POLITICS.

....

....

....

OVER 200 DINERS BECAME ILL AFTER INGESTING THE SPOILED FOOD.

....

....

....

AIR TRAVELERS COULD BE TOLERATING LONG DELAYS THIS WEEKEND.

....

....

....

Negative Verbs

The word "NOT" is an indication that you may have a negative verb. Quite often, finding a positive replacement will result in a more direct sentence.

Here's the negative example:

THREE OTHER CONVICTS <u>DECIDED NOT TO ESCAPE</u> WITH THE FIRST GROUP.

And rewriting the verb makes it positive:

THREE OTHER CONVICTS <u>STAYED</u> BEHIND.

▶ **EXERCISE 3-B**

Revising Negative Verbs

Review these examples. Change negative ones to positive.

THE COUNTY <u>WILL NOT PROHIBIT</u> NEW BUILDING PERMITS.

....

....

THE COUNCIL ADVISED MERCHANTS NOT TO FOLLOW THE LAW.

....

....

THE JURY DID NOT FIND THE DEFENDANT GUILTY.

....

....

THE PILOTS UNION DID NOT ACCEPT THE AGREEMENT.

....

....

THE FRENCH STRIKERS DID NOT WANT THE NEW PENSION LAWS.

....

....

Overwrought Adjectives

For adjectives, the advice is much the same: Keep it simple. Use direct, strong words and rework hyphenated adjectives. For instance, change UNADORNED to PLAIN and POVERTY-STRICKEN to POOR.

▶ **EXERCISE 3-C**

Replacing Overwrought Adjectives

Rewrite with shorter, more powerful adjectives.

POLICE FOUND THE ANTAGONISTIC CROCODILE IN THE PARK'S LAKE.

....

....

....

THE DEFENDANT ADMITTED HE WAS REMORSEFUL.

....

....

....

THE NEWLY MODIFIED HOME APPEARED GARGANTUAN.

....

....

....

AN EXTENSIVE JOURNEY WAS STILL AHEAD.

....

....

....

THE COAST GUARD SAID THE TANKER HAD A TREACHEROUS CARGO.

....

....

....

Watch Out for Sensational Language and/or Loaded Words

Because we need to write for informal speech, encountering opinionated adjectives, sensational adverbs, zany nouns, or the bizarre opinions of secondary sources is a common occurrence for broadcast journalists. Quite often the streetwise adjective or noun colors the meaning and needs elimination or replacement. Here are a few phrases with questionable adjectives:

"THE RECALL PRONE S-U-V"

"THE TROUBLED HEALTH REFORM LAW"

"THE CONTROVERSIAL POLICE DRUG LAB"

"PUZZLING AFGHAN PRESIDENT HAMID KARZAI"

"THE BUMBLING LAWMAKERS"

▶ **EXERCISE 3-D**

Be Vigilant for Loaded Words

Review this example and discuss whether the writer is slanting the story:

WEST POINT POLICE ARE REVIEWING THE FATAL SHOOTING OF A LOVABLE FAMILY PET BY OFFICERS RESPONDING TO A HOME BURGLAR ALARM.

THE 12-YEAR-OLD GOLDEN RETRIEVER HAPPY CONFRONTED PATROLMAN BENNY WILLIAMS IN THE RESIDENCE'S BACKYARD. WILLIAMS SHOT THE ELDERLY AND AFFECTIONATE CANINE THREE TIMES.

HAPPY'S OWNER MARY ANN FOWLER SAID HAPPY WAS ALWAYS FRIENDLY AND WOULD NEVER HARM A SOUL. SHE SAID HER FAMILY IS THINKING OF SUING THE GUN-HAPPY POLICE OVER THE LOSS OF THEIR LOYAL DOG.

► **EXERCISE 3-E**

Be Vigilant for Sensational Words

Discuss these sentences with an eye to revising adjectives (and nouns).

FREE-SPENDING BILLIONAIRE REPUBLICAN SENATE CANDIDATE REGGIE BARNES IS WOOING THE LATINO COMMUNITY BY RUNNING ADS ON SPANISH LANGUAGE TELEVISION NOVELLAS.

THIS IS PART OF A CRAFTY BARNES CAMPAIGN TO REEL IN MORE LATINO SUPPORTERS. FOR MONTHS . . . SPANISH-SPEAKING BARNES OPERATIVES HAVE APPEARED ON SPANISH-LANGUAGE MEDIA TALK SHOWS . . . TOUTING THEIR CANDIDATE.

NEXT WEEK . . . THE UNIVISION NETWORK WILL BEGIN TWO ONE-HOUR SIT-DOWN CONVERSATIONS WITH BARNES . . . THE ONLY INTERVIEWS DONE IN BARNES'S OPULENT BEVERLY HILLS ESTATE.

Slangy Buzzwords or Jargon

Although conversational writing suggests informality, you should be careful to limit the overuse of faddish or clichéd buzzwords that derive from current news situations, teen jargon, sports lingo, pop culture observations, or Internet abbreviations. Examples might be words such as dysfunctional, go the distance, LOL, and so on. This caution also relates to police or legal jargon. Any of these expressions may only appeal to a small portion of your audience.

▶ **EXERCISE 3-F**

Rewriting to Limit Jargon

Rewrite these sentences to make them more easily understood:

ENGINEERS PLAN TO <u>OPERATIONALIZE</u> THE PLANT THIS WEEK.

....

....

....

THE STARTUPS' FOUNDERS SAID THEY COULDN'T MONETIZE THEIR IDEAS.

....

....

....

IT WAS MISSION CRITICAL DAY FOR THE COUNTY KENNEL.

....

....

....

THE ORGANIZERS GAVE A BIG SHOUT-OUT TODAY TO THE FAITHFUL.

....

....

....

THE STATE'S LAWMAKERS SAID THE BILL WOULD LEVEL THE PLAYING FIELD.

....

....

....

O-M-G MIGHT HAVE BEEN THE REACTION TODAY WHEN THE TRANSIT DISTRICT UNVEILED THE NEW HYBRID BUS.

....

....

....

Limit Wordplay

Wordplay is the clever use of themed adjectives or verbs in particular stories. Often called puns, these expressions are effective only when used sparingly. Because they are a challenge to write, there is a temptation to overload a story. Here's an example:

> THERE'S BAD NEWS BREWING FOR COFFEE DRINKERS.
> THE PRICE OF A CUP OF JOE IS GOING UP.
> THE GROUNDS FOR THIS PRICE HIKE ARE NEW LABOR AGREE-
> MENTS IN BRAZIL.
> INDUSTRY OFFICIALS SAY IT WON'T TAKE A LATTE TIME FOR
> THESE COSTS TO PERCOLATE DOWN TO US.
> OUR WALLETS SHOULD FEEL THE JOLT IN TWO MONTHS.

Cut Out Unnecessary Words and Phrases

Redundant words or short descriptive or possessive phrases are often unneeded and can be removed without changing the story's clarity. In many cases, the writer might be using six words where four would do, and common sense will tell you if words can be excised. Here's an example:

> THE COUNCIL VOTED TO REPAVE THE DOWNTOWN DISTRICTS' MANY STREETS.

Change that to

> THE COUNCIL VOTED TO REPAVE THE DOWNTOWN STREETS.

▶ **EXERCISE 3-G**

Eliminate Unnecessary Parts and Simplify

Revise the sentences in this story to eliminate words or phrases if possible:

> THE POLICE UNION'S NEGOTIATING COUNCIL MEMBERS SAY THEY ARE NOW HOPEFUL AND OPTIMISTIC.
> THE COMMENTS CAME AFTER A MARATHON DISCUSSION THAT WENT PAST MIDNIGHT UNTIL THREE A-M IN THE EARLY MORNING.
> FINALLY . . . BOTH SIDES EMERGED FROM THE NON-STOP LENGTHY MEETING AT THE COUNTY OFFICES TO SAY THEY WOULD PUT OFF THE STRIKE FOR AN-OTHER FIVE DAYS AND CONTINUE THE ALL-DAY 24-HOUR TALKS.
> THE CITY'S NEGOTIATING REPRESENTATIVES DECLARED THEY WERE HOPEFUL.

Use a Variety of Words

If possible, a good writer avoids word repetition in sentences or paragraphs. Newswriters should always be on the lookout for duplication and find ways to avoid it.

Here's an example:

> THE FIRE TRUCKS ARRIVED ON ELM STREET AS THE FIRE ROARED OUT THE HOTEL'S FIRST FLOOR WINDOWS.
> FIREFIGHTERS QUICKLY PULLED RESIDENTS FROM THE FIRE'S PATH AND THEN BATTLED THE FLAMES FOR THE NEXT HOUR.
> THE FIRE WAS OUT AT SIX P-M.

Change that to

> THE FIRE TRUCKS ARRIVED ON ELM STREET AS THE FLAMES ROARED OUT THE HOTEL'S FIRST FLOOR WINDOWS.
> CREWS QUICKLY PULLED FOUR RESIDENTS FROM THE BUILDING AND THEN BATTLED THE BLAZE FOR THE NEXT HOUR.
> IT WAS OUT AT SIX P-M.

Repetition Can Be Useful if Managed Carefully

There are cases when a strategic repetition can add a powerful focus. Repeating a single word shortly after its first use triggers this emphasis. This structure, like wordplay, becomes tedious if overused. Here's the example without repetition.

> THE CITY COUNCIL TODAY PASSED A LAW THAT WILL END SPECULATION IN HOUSING IN PORTLAND.

But if you repeat the word "law," this is the result:

> THE CITY COUNCIL TODAY PASSED A LAW . . . A LAW THAT WILL END SPECULATION IN HOUSING IN PORTLAND.

▶ **EXERCISE 3-H**

Repetition for Emphasis

In each sentence, use repetition to emphasize the underlined word:

BIGTOWN STEEL EMPLOYEES ARE SETTING A <u>GOAL</u> TO PRODUCE MORE THAN LAST YEAR'S OUTPUT.

....

....

....

THE JURY RETURNED A GUILTY VERDICT. IT WAS SEEN AS A <u>COURAGEOUS</u> ACT BECAUSE OF THREATS DURING THE TRIAL.

....

....

....

THE WARSHIP MADE AN <u>EMOTIONAL</u> HOMECOMING. IT HAD BEEN AT SEA FOR 14 MONTHS.

....

....

....

THE MAYOR SAID THE BUDGET DEFICIT WAS <u>SIGNIFICANT</u> BECAUSE THE CITY HAD NO WAY TO GET THE MONEY.

....

....

....

THE TRIAL JUDGE WARNED THE DECISION WOULD MAKE A LOT OF PEOPLE <u>ANGRY</u> BECAUSE MANY HAD HOPED THE OLD LADY COULD KEEP HER HOME.

....

....

....

Special Case of the Verb "Say"

Although newswriters are urged to find synonyms to add variety, "say" or "said" is one verb that can be repeated. Alternatives such as assert, declare, state, pronounce, vocalize, exclaim, or voice are stodgy, awkward, and often color the delivery of the sentence. Repeat the verb "say" as often as you like.

Here are two paragraphs; the first uses various synonyms, whereas the second uses repetition of the verb to say:

> POLICE STATED THE SUSPECT TURNED AROUND . . . REACHED FOR THE FELT-TIPPED PEN . . . AND MARKED THE WALLS.
> CITY OFFICIALS DECLARED THE GRAFFITI ARTIST KNEW EXACTLY WHAT HE WAS DOING. THEY VOICED DISGUST WITH WHAT THEY CALLED VANDALISM.
> THE PROSECUTOR ANNOUNCED SHE'D ASK FOR A TRIAL.

Instead, you can change that to the following:

> POLICE SAID THE SUSPECT TURNED AROUND . . . REACHED FOR THE FELT-TIPPED PEN . . . AND MARKED THE WALLS.
> CITY OFFICIALS SAID THE GRAFFITI ARTIST KNEW EXACTLY WHAT HE WAS DOING. THE SAID THEY WERE DISGUSTED WITH THE VANDALISM.
> THE PROSECUTOR SAID SHE'D ASK FOR A TRIAL.

Special Case of the Word "That"

Although the word "that" is often needed in prose, it can be eliminated in most conversational writing. The test is to read the sentence aloud and see if the "that" is necessary. For instance, instead of writing

> THE TEAM'S PLAYERS SAID THEY HOPED THAT THEY WOULD WIN.

the "that" can be dropped:

> THE TEAM'S PLAYERS SAID THEY HOPED THEY WOULD WIN.

In the next example, however, the "that" cannot be removed without rewriting the sentence:

> THE BOAT THAT SUNK WAS REGISTERED TO THE MAYOR.

▶ **EXERCISE 3-1**

Comprehensive Rewrite

Examine and rewrite these examples by removing unneeded data, changing complex words, negative verbs, and unneeded phrases, buzzwords, and loaded language:

TWELVE MEMBERS OF THE SHERIFF'S SWAT TEAM PROVIDED ASSISTANCE DURING THE DANGEROUS APPREHENSION OF THE ANGRY BELLIGERENT SUSPECT . . . JOHN E. JUDD . . . 29 . . . OF BELLEVILLE.

....

....

....

OFFICIALS SAID THAT THE VIOLENT STANDOFF TRANSFORMED A NORMALLY TRANQUIL AND PICTURESQUE AGRICULTURAL TOWN INTO A COMMUNITY OF FEAR.

....

....

....

THE EXHILARATED SCIENTISTS WERE UPBEAT . . . DECLARING THAT THE TRAILBLAZING DISCOVERY WAS A HOME RUN OF SORTS IN THE WORLD OF PLANETARY EXPLORATION.

....

....

....

IN AN UNEXPECTED MOVE . . . THE UNRULY GLOBAL WARMING PROTESTORS DID NOT CROSS THE POLICE BARRIERS ON THE STREET BY THE MEETING HALL. INSTEAD . . . THE HOOLIGANS BROKE INTO SMALL KNOTS AND UNLAWFULLY BANGED THEIR SLOGAN-LADEN SIGNS ON THE STORE WINDOWS FACING ALONG THE STREET.

....

....

....

▶ **EXERCISE 3-J**

Cutting Out Words and Making Choices

Try your hand at seeing how few words you can use. Shorten these sentences by simplifying words, deleting unnecessary phrases, and replacing negative verbs.

TWO AS YET UNIDENTIFIED MEN AT THE STARLIGHT MOTEL SUFFERED SERIOUS AND NEAR FATAL INJURIES IN SPECTACULAR FALLS FROM SECOND FLOOR BALCONIES TO THE GROUND FLOOR BELOW. POLICE STATED THAT THEY HAVE NOT YET DEDUCED A MOTIVE.

....

....

....

....

TREASURE HUNTERS WORKING THE CRYSTAL BLUE WATERS OF THE CARIBBEAN SEA ARE DECLARING THAT THEY HAVE CERTAINLY FOUND THE REMAINS OF A SUNKEN 16TH-CENTURY SPANISH FLEET GALLEON CALLED . . . LA GORDITA DE ORO. THE LA GORDITA HAD SAILED BOUND FROM CUBA TO SPAIN BUT WAS LOW HANGING FRUIT FOR ENGLISH PIRATES LIKE THE INFAMOUS CAPTAIN MORGAN.

....

....

....

....

THE BRITISH GOVERNMENT SIGNALED TODAY THAT IT IS READY TO GO THE DISTANCE AND OFFER DIRECT FINANCIAL ASSISTANCE AND SUPPORT TO THE FINANCIALLY STRAPPED AND TROUBLED IRISH GOVERNMENT. THE ANNOUNCEMENT CAME AMIDST THE USUAL CHAOS AT THE MEETING OF 16 EURO-ZONE COUNTRIES.

....

....

....

....

Attribution

Attribution is the inclusion of source identification to establish credibility or doubt in your story. In spoken news, attribution goes first because it verifies authenticity for the material that follows. Whether or not it is needed involves many individual judgments. Following are suggestions to help you determine when attribution is appropriate.

Use It for Credibility

By naming your sources of information, you enable your viewers or listeners to judge the value of your facts. The audience knows a foreign policy statement that originates at the White House has more credibility than a foreign policy statement from the manager of the local supermarket. In stories with contested facts, attributions let the audience decide about credibility.

Use It to Show Doubt

Similarly, if you have doubts about the quality of the information, it is traditional journalistic practice to alert the audience to this fact. Anonymous telephone information inserted in a story should be identified as such. Exclusive stories from other media should credit those organizations, unless you can crosscheck the information. Also, the source for any information from a suspect organization, one with a big name but only four members, must be identified.

Use It to Support Opinion

Attribution is always needed if you are reporting opinion or speculation.

Use It in Crime Stories

Always use attribution in crime stories. Make a point that this information comes from authoritative sources. When describing a crime to which a person's name may be linked, it is irresponsible to forego attribution.

Shorten Attribution or Discard It to Save Space

Here broadcast use is not the same as print. Because story space is limited in newscasts, it is often necessary to condense the source of information or to eliminate it altogether. Often, a writer might exclude the attribution in the case of routine sources that mean little to the outcome of the story. If the Consumer Price Index (CPI) goes up or down, there is little debate where the CPI comes from, so why bother with the attribution.

The Placement for Attribution

Although newspaper and wire service copy traditionally put the attribution at the end of a sentence, broadcast puts it first. Here's an example of print placement.

> "The United States and European officials will soon meet in new negotiations over currency and trade agreements, according to a highly placed state department source."

▶ **EXERCISE 3-K**

Attribution Work

Examine these sentences for attribution problems. Be prepared to discuss if you would use the attribution and how it might be written. If needed, place it first.

A TEAMSTER UNION OFFICIAL IS SAYING THAT ALL GROCERY CLERKS SHOULD GET AT LEAST SIX WEEKS ANNUAL VACATION.

....
....

ALL STATE TROOPERS WILL RECEIVE ETHICS COUNSELING AFTER THE SEX SCANDALS . . . SAYS STATE POLICE CHIEF RAUL RAMIREZ.

....
....

AN EARTHQUAKE SHOOK THE TRI-CITY AREA THIS MORNING . . . REGISTERING THREE-POINT-FOUR ON THE RICHTER SCALE . . . ACCORDING TO THE GEOLOGICAL SERVICE.

....
....

THE REFINERY RELEASED UNTREATED CHEMICALS INTO THE MARSHY WETLANDS . . . ACCORDING TO THE SAVE THE MARSH GROUP.

....
....

BUGS BUNNY WILL BE 50 YEARS OLD TOMORROW . . . A CARTOON OFFICIAL SAID.

....
....

THE SUSPECT IS BYRON WALCOTT . . . ACCORDING TO POLICE.

....
....

In broadcast, the attribution automatically goes first. It allows the audience a chance to judge source credibility as the facts are heard rather than waiting for a delayed attribution.

> A STATE DEPARTMENT OFFICIAL IS SAYING THE U-S AND EUROPEAN OFFICIALS WILL MEET TO DISCUSS CURRENCY AND TRADE AGREEMENTS.

► **EXERCISE 3-L**

Comprehensive Review Including Attribution

Examine these sentences for word complexity, unneeded words and phrases, and attribution problems. If necessary, rewrite for an effective broadcast style.

THE SAN CRISTOBAL MAYOR ACCEPTED AN ILLEGAL BRIBE DURING NEW CONVENTION CENTER WORK . . . THE HERALD IS REPORTING TODAY.

....

....

....

....

A TEAM OF DOCTORS AT THE BENTON CAMPUS STATE UNIVERSITY MEDICAL CENTER WILL ATTEMPT A DIFFICULT BUT NOT IMPOSSIBLE CROSS-SPECIES NERVE TRANSPLANT . . . HOSPITAL OFFICIALS ARE SAYING.

....

....

....

....

RACE OFFICIALS DECLARED THE STREETS AND AVENUES WILL BE CROWDED AND JAMMED WITH UPWARDS OF 40-THOUSAND RUNNERS IN TOMORROW'S MUSCULAR DYSTROPHY MARATHON.

....

....

....

....

Active and Passive Voice

The passive voice, a sentence structure in which the entity or person responsible for the action appears after the verb, is a common roadblock for beginning broadcast writers. Using the passive voice is a leftover from schoolwork that trained us to place an important word or event at the beginning of the sentence.

Following this rule, in writing a story about a bank robbery in which "bank" is the focus word, we habitually insert the word "bank" somewhere in the first three words of the sentence: "THE BANK WAS ROBBED BY THE LONE GUNMAN." This verb is in the passive voice because the action was done to the bank not by the bank.

In broadcast, however, it is important to construct a smooth sentence flow. Start the sentence with whoever does the action, even if a word, such as "bank" is still the story focus. Placing the subject before the verb makes it active voice: "THE LONE GUN-MAN ROBBED THE BANK." It is shorter and more direct. Broadcast writers should make every attempt to keep all the verbs in active rather than passive voice.

Be careful not to confuse voice with tense. Voice has nothing to do with when the action happened, only with the placement of who or what is responsible for the action in relation to the verb. The rule is: Subject-Verb-Object.

Changing the Voice

There are cues to alert you to passive voice. In the passive voice sentence, "The mail carrier was bitten by the dog," the dog is obviously responsible for the action but comes after the verb. The "**was**" and "**by**" are clues that a passive voice verb is there.

Turning a sentence around is easy. Here are some passive voice sentences and the active equivalents.

Passive: THE OIL SPILL WAS SPOTTED BY THE COAST GUARD BOAT.

Active: THE COAST GUARD BOAT SPOTTED THE OIL SPILL.

Passive: THE FAMILY WAS FORCED TO FLEE BY THE FLOOD.

Active: THE FLOOD FORCED THE FAMILY TO FLEE.

In each case, the cues are obvious—"was" and "by." Notice also that the active voice sentence is shorter and the action flows more smoothly. You are saving words and time.

Passive: MILLIONS OF DOLLARS WORTH OF ARMS HAVE BEEN SHIPPED TO THE TERRORISTS BY THE SECRET GROUPS IN ARGENTINA.

Active: SECRET GROUPS IN ARGENTINA HAVE SHIPPED MILLIONS OF DOLLARS WORTH OF ARMS TO THE TERRORISTS.

▶ **EXERCISE 3-M**

Replacing Passive Voice

Now, change these passive voice verbs to active.

THREE HOMES AND A SCHOOL ARE BEING THREATENED BY GRASS FIRES OUT-
SIDE OF TUCSON.

....

....

OVER 100 WORKERS AT THE XERXES METALS PLANT WILL BE LAID OFF BY THE
COMPANY BEGINNING NEXT WEDNESDAY.

....

....

THE FAMOUS JET CAR USED IN THE BATMAN SERIES WAS AMONG 50 AUCTIONED
OFF IN CHICAGO BY A COLLECTOR.

....

....

FOUR SURFERS WERE ATTACKED BY A GREAT WHITE SHARK OFF THE SANTA
CRUZ COAST.

....

....

THE RECORD WAS BROKEN BY AMTRAK'S NEW ACELA HIGH-SPEED TRAIN.

....

....

THE SUNDAY NEWS HAS LEARNED A MOVE IS BEING MADE BY CLAY COUNTY
OFFICIALS TO STOP CONSTRUCTION OF THE NEW TRI-CITY LIGHT RAIL PROJECT.
AS A RESULT . . . THE CONTRACTORS WILL BE ASKED TO ABANDON PRELIMI-
NARY WORK ON THE MUCH-DELAYED SYSTEM.

....

....

More Dynamic Verb Forms

Verbs that are grammatically correct might need a makeover to add a dynamic touch. For instance, if a an institutional policy is not over and is continuing, you can replace the simple present tense with the participial form, adding an "ing" ending. Here's an example:

BANKS <u>CHARGE</u> 12-PERCENT INTEREST FOR THREE MONTHS ON THE CONTROVERSIAL LOANS.

Because this story is about an ongoing policy, you can strengthen the verb:

BANKS <u>ARE CHARGING</u> 12-PERCENT INTEREST FOR THREE MONTHS ON THE CONTROVERSIAL LOANS.

Here are more examples:

TRANSPORTATION SAFETY BOARD WORKERS <u>ARE SEARCHING</u> THE WRECKAGE OF THE AIRLINER TONIGHT . . . LOOKING FOR THE CAUSE OF THE CRASH.
THE CITY COUNCIL <u>IS BETTING</u> THAT THE NORTH STATE UTILITY GROUP WON'T RAISE THE RATES.

In broadcast, you can also use the participial form to reflect future actions:

THE CITY ATTORNEY WILL BE TAKING THE STATE TO COURT OVER THE LATEST LAW ON RENT CONTROLS.

Or

THE CITY ATTORNEY WILL BE FILING THAT LAWSUIT NEXT WEEK WHEN THE COURTS REOPEN.

▶ **EXERCISE 3-N**

Using "ING" Verb Forms

Examine these sentences with an eye to making your verbs more dynamic. Rewrite if necessary.

CORAL GABLES CLOSED ITS MARINA ENTRANCE AFTER YESTERDAY'S TOUR BOAT ACCIDENT.

....
....
....
....
....
....

THE FLOODS THAT SWEPT THROUGH BIRNEY FALLS YESTERDAY CAUSED PROBLEMS TODAY.

....
....
....
....
....
....

POLITICAL CRITICS SUGGESTED THE SENATOR SHOULD LAY LOW FOR A WHILE UNTIL THE TAXPAYERS BACKLASH SUBSIDES.

....
....
....
....
....
....

▶ **EXERCISE 3-O**

Immediacy Needs

In each case, rewrite the verbs if there is a continuing action or policy:

THE ZOO BOARD WILL GIVE A THREE-MONTH PASS TO EVERYONE WHO AT-TENDS TODAY'S EXHIBITION.

....

....

....

....

DOCTORS HOPED THE INJECTIONS LAST NIGHT WILL SAVE THE VICTIM FROM INFECTION.

....

....

....

....

THE WANDERING WHALE ENTERED THE EAST RIVER AND MARINE MAMMAL EXPERTS CONTINUED TO WATCH ITS PROGRESS.

....

....

....

....

UNIVERSITY OFFICIALS WILL TAKE A WAIT-AND-SEE ATTITUDE AFTER THE COACH'S LATEST OUTBURST.

....

....

....

....

Common Reference Problems

The need for tightly condensed broadcast copy often results in unclear pronoun references. Any pronoun that is ambiguous must be cleared up.

Pronouns

Broadcast writers often use pronouns with confusing antecedents. If the pronoun's reference isn't clear, rewrite the sentence to repeat the proper name and eliminate the pronouns. Sometimes this will result in a longer sentence. Here are two examples:

> THE GOVERNOR AND THE ASSEMBLY SPEAKER DISCUSSED THE SITUATION. THEN HE MADE A MOVE TO CUT THE BUDGET.

For this example, both the governor and the speaker were men. Therefore, it is necessary to identify the antecedent to the pronoun "<u>he</u>" or the sentence is confusing. Here's the rewrite:

> THE GOVERNOR AND THE ASSEMBLY SPEAKER DISCUSSED THE SITUATION . . . THEN THE <u>GOVERNOR</u> MADE A MOVE TO CUT THE BUDGET.

Here's a second example of unclear reference:

> POLICE ARRESTED FIVE MEMBERS OF THE PROTEST GROUP AND SAID THEY ARE EXHAUSTED AFTER SPENDING ALL DAY AT THE DEMONSTRATION.

Who is tired here? The police or the protestors? Identify the "they." Here's the rewrite:

> POLICE ARRESTED FIVE MEMBERS OF THE PROTEST GROUP AND SAID THE DEMONSTRATORS ARE TIRED AFTER SPENDING ALL DAY AT THE EVENT.

▶ **EXERCISE 3-P**

Pronoun Reference

Correct ambiguous pronoun references in these sentences.

THE SUPREME COURT HAS OVERTURNED A LOWER COURT DEATH PENALTY RULING. THIS IS CONSIDERED A LANDMARK IN PENAL LAW.

....

....

....

....

THE DOG SHOW IS TOUGH ON BOTH JUDGES AND THE CONTESTANTS. THEY HAVE TO SIT QUIETLY FOR HOURS.

....

....

....

....

RATS CARRIED THE PLAGUE IN THE MIDDLE AGES . . . AND NOW EPIDEMIOLO-GISTS ARE SAYING THEY ARE RESPONSIBLE FOR THE MYSTERIOUS ILLNESSES IN NEW MEXICO.

....

....

....

....

AFTER THE OIL SPILL . . . THE SHIP'S OWNERS FIRED THE CAPTAIN AND THE FIRST MATE . . . ENDING A 35-YEAR CAREER WITH THE COMPANY.

....

....

....

....

Chapter Summary

A broadcast newswriter must always strive for the most concise word choice and most direct sentence order. Shifting scripts to spoken news requires attention to critical areas including verb and adjective simplicity, jargon and buzzwords, repetition, attribution, active voice, and pronoun reference.

Writing Lead Sentences

4

Broadcast lead sentences are a critical element with a dual purpose. They must attract the widest audience to the story and, at the same time, set off a carefully constructed narrative account.

Lead sentences, sometimes called "ledes," come in many different flavors. For major breaking news, the lead sentence can be simple and obvious; but in minor stories, second-day stories, features, or those with video, writers often use devices such as irony, common wisdom, or the unexpected angle to craft the lead. This chapter explores strategies for lead sentences.

Glossary

BREAKING NEWS An unexpected event that requires coverage.

CLICHÉ LEAD A lead sentence that relies on tired or trite phrasing.

COMMON WISDOM A generally accepted account of something, usually without scientific proof.

EXCEPTION LEAD A lead sentence that focuses on an unexpected turn of events.

FEATURE OR SOFT LEAD A lead sentence for a story that does not involve timely or deadline information.

FOLO LEAD (for follow-up). A lead sentence that advances and updates the information of a new or breaking story.

IMMEDIACY CUE Word or phrase that adds a heightened sense of urgency to a story. Examples would be "This just in" or "At this moment."

INTENSITY LEAD A lead sentence that emphasizes the story impact and offers little information.

IRONY A narrative device that focuses on the opposite of the expected result or meaning.

PERSPECTIVE LEAD A lead sentence that relates the current story to previous events or trends.

REAX LEAD (for reaction). A lead that emphasizes the responses of persons or groups to previous stories.

SEGUE A transition. In news, the segue lead ties a story to the preceding story.

Broadcast Leads Never Tell the Whole Story

A lead sentence in broadcast is far more complex and critical than it is in a print or online. The newspaper has a headline to attract the eye and a lead sentence to begin the story; in broadcast, the single lead sentence must do both, drawing the audience to the story topic while beginning the narrative. Broadcast leads attempt to get every viewer engaged with each story. It is crucial that the broadcast lead be clever, tight, attractive, and informative.

In some print stylebooks, papers allow the writer to summarize the entire story in the lead sentence, the so-called inverted pyramid. But for broadcast and online spoken news, this is never the case. Instead, broadcast stories start slowly and release bits of information a little at a time, until the story finishes with the future. Picture the news story as a rock rolling down a hill. Each time it rotates, it reveals another part of the story.

Broadcast lead sentences require only a few details, generally the "**what**" and the "**where.**" The "who" and the "why" come later. The "when" will either be highlighted or ignored.

One Night's Lead Sentences

Here are some leads from the first 20 minutes of a local broadcast newscast. They represent the categories of lead sentences we will study.

IT IS CONSIDERED ONE OF THE MOST DANGEROUS CITIES IN THE BAY AREA AND TODAY POLICE WARNED IT COULD GET WORSE. (perspective)

POLICE SAY A NIGHT OF TEQUILA DRINKING MAY EXPLAIN WHY A TODDLER WAS FOUND LAST NIGHT ON THE STREETS OF A NORTH BAY CITY. (new story)

PROSECUTORS HAVE RESTED THEIR CASE IN THE JOHANNES MESHERLE TRIAL. (folo)

FLAGS AT THE STATE CAPITOL WILL FLY AT HALF STAFF TOMOR-ROW. (intensity)

LONGSHOREMEN ARE UNLOADING THAT CONTROVERSIAL ISRAELI SHIP TODAY. (folo)

RUSSIAN PRESIDENT DIMITRI MEDGEVED WILL TOUR LOCAL TECH PLANTS TODAY. (new story)

HER LIFE NEARLY ENDED SUDDENLY BUT THANKS TO A SHERIFFS DEPUTY . . . THIS TWO YEAR OLD IS ALIVE TODAY. (feature)

GOOD THINGS COME TO THOSE WHO RECYCLE. (common wisdom)

YOUR CHILDS DOCTOR MAY BE MAKING MORE MISTAKES THAN YOU THINK. (exception)

SOME LOCAL MUSICIANS GOT TO REPRESENT OUR AREA IN SHANG-HAI. (new story)

TODAY IS THE FIRST DAY OF SUMMER . . . BUT THERE IS A MOVE ON IN ONE COASTAL CITY TO RESTRICT RENTALS ALONG THE BEACH. (perspective)

WE ALL KNOW THE CURRENT BUDGET SITUATION IN THE STATE CAPITOL IS ROCKY BUT TODAY THERE WERE COMPLAINTS ABOUT ANOTHER TYPE OF ROCK. (segue from previous story about state government)

What Might Interest an Audience About This Story? Trust Yourself

Suppose there is a story about new research on mammals and underwater communications. The writer should explore the usual suspects: the effect on the viewers, proximity, prominence, and finally human interest. But if that doesn't pan out, another tack is to read the material and underline key words or phrases that are intriguing.

Here's an example of the story situation notes with key ideas highlighted.

Situation Notes

Handout from local sea park on dolphins and theories of communication.

From: Researchers at the Saltmarsh Sea Mammal Park (very close to your city).

Scientists at Saltmarsh Park have now completed a seven-year study and have concluded that <u>dolphins communicate</u> for playful as well as <u>serious reasons</u>. In the past, researchers thought that the mammals only used their <u>underwater squeaks and whistles</u> to <u>warn of danger</u> or suggest food availability. Now . . . the new research at Saltmarsh seems to indicate that adult dolphins <u>play games to pass the time</u> at sea. Dr. Bivalve Watson led the research. It was conducted at the sea park as well as in the waters off Brazil.

Suppose a writer tried this lead. It refers to the story and although accurate, it is lifeless and uninteresting.

SCIENTISTS AT THE SALTMARSH SEA PARK HAVE SOME NEW RESEARCH ABOUT DOLPHINS.

With this lead, you are really saying "SCIENTISTS ARE DOING THEIR JOB." You won't engage a wide audience with this dreary start. You need to lock onto a better angle. It's time to trust your own curiosity. What topics excite the researchers in this story? What piques your curiosity? It could be a new detail, a bold jump in knowledge, a risk taken, or perhaps irony. Did the scientists do anything extraordinary to debunk an older theory? If you can isolate this, you'll have the topic area for your lead.

The key ideas should lead to triggers for an audience's interest. As an example, in the fifth line of the situation notes, note the key words "play games." This phrase could be the inspiration. Put that in or near the lead. Try this rewrite:

SOME LOCAL SCIENTISTS ARE SAYING DOLPHINS COMMUNICATE FOR SOCIAL REASONS . . . SUCH AS PLAYING GAMES.

That's better. Elements that intrigued you are now in this lead. This might attract not only people generally interested in the sea park but also those who like marine biology, our relationships with other creatures on the planet, or with our attempts to communicate with them.

Caution: Avoid Sensationalism or Hype in the Leads

A television station in a major California market once had an unwritten but well-known policy that urged its newswriters to insert either immediacy cues or adjectives such as "bizarre," "stunning," "spectacular," or "one-of-a-kind" into almost every lead. The stories all sounded like this:

THE U-S STATE DEPARTMENT . . . IN A STUNNING MOVE . . . IS GOING TO . . .

The constant use of these **immediacy cues** crosses that line into sensationalism or hype, which is the repeated use of certain elements to thrill or amaze. At some point, this repetition desensitizes the audience.

If you have stories that are indeed bizarre, you don't need to hype them. Your audience will catch on if your lead gives away enough of the story.

Eight Categories of Leads

There are many different approaches to crafting a lead sentence. Although it is difficult to sort leads into categories, we will now consider those that occur most often: the intensity, new story, reax, update or folo, perspective, exception, segue, and feature leads.

The Impact or Intensity Lead

This lead focuses on the power or influence of the story. It postpones most facts, except proximity, for later. Impact leads can work for any type of powerful story—from breaking news to features. Ten percent of a newscast might be impact leads. Here are a few examples:

THEY DID SOMETHING TODAY ON WALL STREET THAT KNOCKED THEIR SOCKS OFF ACROSS THE COUNTRY.

FLAGS WILL FLY AT HALF STAFF TODAY IN THE STATE CAPITOL.

DOWNTOWN COMMUTERS SHOULD PREPARE FOR THE WORST.

THE STATE'S TAXPAYERS AREN'T GOING TO LIKE THIS.

IT'S THE MERGER TO END ALL MERGERS.

SCIENTISTS ARE CALLING IT A MAJOR BREAKTHROUGH.

STUDENTS AT CARSON ELEMENTARY WON'T FORGET THIS ONE.

These are effective leads if they deliver. The dangers in impact leads are hype and sensationalism. A rather tepid story following an impact lead can discourage your audience and reduce your credibility.

► **EXERCISE 4-A**

Write an Impact Lead From This Situation

Situation Notes

The U.S. government has announced it will spend up to one trillion dollars to build a high-speed rail network over the next 20 years. The trains will connect 32 of the most populous cities and cut the current rail travel times by over 50 percent.

New Story (Breaking News) Leads

New story leads are the straightforward variety used for unexpected items. Their attraction lies in the novelty of the story topic or line. This could be a sudden event, a scientific report, a crime story, or any action on topic that hasn't been heard before. Whatever the theme, the new story lead is the first time that the audience will hear about this story.

Including only a few details in a new story lead is generally enough to engage the audience's interest. Here's an example of the "what" and the "where" in a lead:

A MAN DROVE HIS CAR THROUGH A DOWNTOWN GREAT FALLS BANK WINDOW.

In this lead, the writer is offering a few facts to hint at the item's unique nature but is saving the identification (who), the results in injuries and damages (what), and the reason (why) for the central part of the story.

▶ **EXERCISE 4-B**

Writing New Story Leads

New story leads might account for a quarter of your stories. Because the goal is to release only a few details, the new story leads can be short and to the point. Write new story lead sentences for these situations and keep the word count to 11 words or under.

Situation Notes 1

You use a reporter's notes that the Municipal Transit District is now planning to spend $2,500,000 to redesign and rebuild some of the 80 new hybrid buses they purchased last year.

The work will start in one month.

Although the new hybrids had been planned to replace the aging diesel fleet, many transmissions on the new buses broke down and are now out of service. That leaves the district short on running stock.

When the repairs begin, service for commuters to downtown and back will be curtailed even further, meaning delays of up to an hour on some lines.

With a few calls, you learn that the work is being done because of a Transit District mistake in ordering the buses. The wrong gear ratios were selected and the stress destroyed many of the gearboxes.

....

....

....

Situation Notes 2

At their regular Tuesday meeting, your county's Board of Supervisors heard a report about a toxic substance on the tile surfaces of the McDermott Park public swimming pool. Health Director Shirley McClean suggested draining the pool and having it scrubbed. The supervisors are worried about doing this because summer vacation will start next week and the pool will be busy every day. Then the county attorney informed the supervisors they would be liable if anyone became ill from any toxic substance. Supervisors voted 5-0 to close the pool for one week. The McDermott Park pool serves an area of nearly 40,000 residents.

Situation Notes 3

A sinkhole has opened up overnight in your city, taking with it a major bridge approach road while damaging two houses and a tire repair shop. The traffic disruption means drivers will have to detour to a bridge over a mile away. Two houses on the edge of the sinkhole have been red tagged and the families told to evacuate. The tire shop is halfway into the hole and is a total loss. There are 15 cars in or partially in the sinkhole. They had been parked along the curb.

The chasm is almost 200 feet long and 30 feet wide. At some spots, it is nearly 20 feet deep. City civil engineers say it is the result of an underground aquifer that flooded this year due to late heavy rains. At this point, they have no plans on how to fix it.

Reax Leads

This is a strong lead to update any story less than a day old. Basically, a **reax** lead advances the story by opening with the reaction of someone who comments on the initial event. To find that person, ask: Who will be affected? Get a response from that person and it becomes the lead. Then you follow the lead sentence with a background of the initial event.

An example would be if your city manager began the process to fire the local transit district director. Even if that was done at a late-night meeting and you are uncertain whether your audience has heard about it or read it online or in the paper, your broadcast lead the next morning might not be the firing as much as the reaction (reax) to the firing. It's both an update and an advance to the story. Here's the reax lead on that one.

SOME OF TWIN FALL'S BUS DRIVERS SAY THEY ARE UNHAPPY THEIR BOSS IS NOW OUT OF A JOB . . . etc.

The next paragraph explains what happened; then in the fourth or fifth graph, return to the reaction. The reax lead is a good choice, because of the need to advance to the information.

► **EXERCISE 4-C**

Reax Leads

Review each situation and continue the reax lead. Keep your leads under 11 words.

Situation A (for the 6 pm newscast)

A Tea Party candidate declares she will oppose the Republican incumbent in the primary. This may mean the defeat of an influential longtime GOP loyalist.

....

....

....

....

Situation B (for the 9 pm newscast)

By 7 pm that night, the local Republican county chairman has organized a press conference and denounced the Tea Party candidate, saying the GOP needs to remain unified to win.

REPUBLICAN LEADERS ARE ANGRY . . . (fill in the rest)

....

....

....

....

....

Situation C (for the 11 pm newscast the next morning)

At 9:30, your reporter has located and interviewed the Democratic candidate, Maxine DelRay. She is delighted with the opposition's split.

(write your own lead here)

....

....

....

....

Folo, Second-Day, or Update Leads

All news stories have a life span. If it is a local warehouse fire, it might be two days; if it is the massive BP oil well blowout, it could go 100 days. For each of these, there are some predicable follow-ups. A folo, second-day, or update lead advances this earlier story. These leads are focused on the next step, whether it is an investigation, explanation, action taken by government, and so on. These differ from the reax because these are not based on a personal reaction to the story.

Although the folo and update leads highlight the same information, there is a slight difference. Updates can come at any time. The second-day lead is usually the beginning of the major newscast the next day.

This type of lead presents the problem of estimating how much background the public remembers and how much is needed to brief them.

AN APPEALS COURT HAS REVERSED AN IMPORTANT RULING IN THE FLORIDA ELECTION CASE.

Your listeners or viewers may not be familiar with which court decision you are talking about. A better lead reveals a topic to the ruling.

AN APPEALS COURT HAS REVERSED A FLORIDA ORDER TO RECOUNT DAMAGED BALLOTS IN SEMINOLE COUNTY.

► **EXERCISE 4-D**

Second-Day, Folos, or Updates

Review these news situations and write a lead sentence that advances each story. Keep your lead to 11 words, if possible.

Situation Notes

BERNOULLI, France . . . A 270 foot unsinkable ferryboat capsized and sank yesterday in choppy seas in the mouth of the harbor at Oostende, Belgium.

All 37 passengers and the crew of six were rescued. The ferryboat had just completed a trip from Dover, England, and now is resting on its side in only 40 feet of water. It is a hazard to navigation, authorities conceded.

Today, officials are closing the usually busy Oostende harbor until they decide what to do about the sunken ferryboat. The harbor serves as the principal ferry terminal for boats from Britain.

....
....
....
....
....
....

Situation Notes

DRY FORK, Montana . . . The three-day-old 100,000 acre Yellowstone wildfire that has scorched isolated timberlands for the past week has suddenly jumped containment lines and is heading for some well-known park sites.

Fire control officials say the flames could endanger the western campgrounds and the Old Faithful geyser area if they continue on their current path.

Authorities are already closing down those areas of the park and have a plan to evacuate tourists if the fire line gets closer.

....
....
....
....
....
....

Perspective Leads

Perspective is overview—a comparison with current situations, the past, or other associated material or its inclusion in some recognizable pattern—and it is the journalist's job to provide perspective if needed for each story. In newspapers, that may come several paragraphs after the lead, but in broadcast it's more common to find perspective in the lead because a perspective lead most closely resembles the opening of a conversation, for which a person might say "Well, it's happened again."

Quite often the perspective on the story is what makes it interesting. By placing perspective in the lead, you are alerting the audience right away to the most intriguing element. To write a perspective lead, you ignore the immediacy, the new reax, or the update on the item. Instead, you begin with the overview—how this event fits into the pattern. To find the perspective, ask yourself

• **Is this story related to current controversies or other events?**

For example, even if you have new information about one of many buildings burned in today's flash brush fire, your lead might ignore it. Instead, the lead will wrap various damage reports together, giving a perspective on the growing tragedy.

FIRE OFFICIALS ARE NOW SAYING THE ROGERS FLAT FIRE IS THE BIGGEST IN TEN YEARS.

• **Does this topic fit into any historical pattern?**

For example, if this story is about a monkey that has escaped from the local zoo, and you know there have been a number of escapes, then you might choose to bypass the new story lead and go instead with the perspective lead.

Here's a new story lead, usable but dull, because it doesn't have perspective.

A MONKEY ESCAPED FROM THE STEELTOWN ZOO THIS MORNING

A perspective lead relates today's event to a pattern.

FOR THE THIRD TIME THIS MONTH . . . A STEELTOWN ZOO MONKEY IS ON THE LOOSE.
IT ESCAPED FROM THE MONKEY ISLAND EXHIBIT SOMETIME THIS MORNING.

Perspective leads are popular. Only one word of caution: Do not add perspective if you haven't researched the facts or don't understand the situation. A cardinal rule of journalism—"Don't Assume Anything"—is never more important than here. Check your facts carefully.

▶ **EXERCISE 4-E**

Perspective Leads

Review the situation notes and write the lead perspective sentence. Your leads should be no more than 11 words long.

Situation Notes 1

Three days of torrential rain. Serious flooding now. By making calls to the suburbs of Steeltown, you've found three newsworthy items.

1. In Carrington Falls, a canyon flooded and two houses were completely lost. No injuries.

2. In East Merimac, a drainage culvert backed up and millions of gallons of runoff flooded the Eastvale shopping center. Water is three feet deep. No injuries but 24 stores affected and millions in damage.

3. In Bestwicke, a house slid down a hillside and crumbled the back wall of a cookie store on the street below. No one was hurt.

....

....

....

....

....

Situation Notes 2

No negotiations today and none scheduled tomorrow. This is now the 45th day of the first hospital workers strike in Brayer County in 10 years. Local 231 of the Hospital Workers wants a 4 percent raise, but the county says it cannot allow any pay hikes this year. There are 600 workers out at four locations. Only doctors are working at the hospitals and only emergency services are offered.

....

....

....

....

....

Exception or Irony Leads

The exception to the normal routine is a commonly used lead.

The exception lead reflects the one-of-a-kind nature of the situation. All you need to ask is, "Is this unusual or somehow outside of the normal routine for this event?"

For instance . . . a zoo shuttle bus driver on her first day makes a wrong turn and ends up inside the giraffe enclosure from which she has to call for help. The lead sounds like this:

NORMALLY . . . THE ELEPHANT TRAIN AT THE ZOO STAYS OUTSIDE
THE CAGES . . . BUT TODAY WAS DIFFERENT.

The irony lead comes into play when something happens that is <u>exactly</u> opposite of what is expected:

NORMALLY . . . PIGS LIVE OUTSIDE.
BUT IN MAR VISTA ESTATES . . . LUANN MELTON SHARES HER SUB-
URBAN HOME WITH HER POT-BELLIED COMPANION . . . PORKY.

▶ **EXERCISE 4-F**

Exception or Irony Leads

Write exception or irony leads for the following situations. Keep your lead to 11 words or less.

A commuter airline pilot became confused while on approach in Ft. Lauderdale and landed at the wrong airport.

....

....

....

....

A bank mistakenly deposited extra money in a retired man's account. When he went looking for his usual $1,500, he had $1,500,000.

....

....

....

....

Swallows usually nest in the recesses of roof eaves around the city, but this year one bird happily set up a nest in a streetlight that hangs over the major intersection.

....

....

....

....

....

City gardeners usually ride on large, gas-powered mowers to cut the park grass but this year they have brought in a herd of goats.

....

....

....

....

....

A mother dog has adopted a stray kitten as part of its litter.

....

....

....

....

....

A group of seniors from the Westfield Retirement Home went skydiving. Everyone who participated was over 75.

....

....

....

....

....

Segue Leads

A segue is a music term describing the transition interval between songs. It is used as a noun to describe a transition ("had a tight segue") or as a verb ("to segue from X to Y"). In news, the term describes the transition from one story to the next.

A **segue** lead for story B would be based on key themes the previous story A. The producer makes this happen by clustering similar stories. Once the story rundown is locked, it's possible to write a segue lead where contiguous stories have the same themes.

The segue lead can be based on story conditions as well as time or location. Sometimes the segues are easy and flow naturally from the previous story. But often you may have to look hard for key ideas in story A to make that leap to story B.

Here's an example. The previous story A is about an escaped rhesus monkey. The story that follows, story B, is about the arrival of new pandas at the zoo.

ZOOKEEPERS HAD A MUCH MORE PLEASANT EXPERIENCE TODAY
WHEN TWO RARE PANDAS . . .

That example allowed story B to spin off some information from the story before it. But suppose your producer wants the segue to be related in a different way. Story A is still the zoo story, but story B is about a prison escape. It might be farfetched but that depends on how you handle it. Here's an example of a segue lead for story B:

AN ESCAPE OF A DIFFERENT NATURE . . . AND FAR MORE DANGEROUS
. . . AT COUNTY JAIL . . .

Geographic or time segues are most common and are often added later by a newscaster. Here's a geographic example for the prison escape:

ALSO IN BRAYER COUNTY . . . TWO MEN WHO . . . etc.

The danger of segue leads. The segue lead's biggest trap is the attempt to make a connection that is tenuous at best or not there at all. That's happened too many times in news. Here's an actual segue lead from a network radio broadcast. It followed a story about a Mexican hurricane named Richard.

AND FROM HURRICANE RICHARD TO KEITH RICHARDS.

The remainder of the story was about the Rolling Stones member's new book. If the first story had been dropped, the lead would make no sense.

▶ **EXERCISE 4-G**

Writing Segue Leads

Your job is to read story A and then write a segue lead for story B. Your lead should be no more than 11 words long.

Story A

COMMUTERRAIL WILL BE SLOWING DOWN THE MORNING TRAIN SERVICE FROM MAR VISTA ESTATES TO STEELTOWN.

TRANSIT OFFICIALS SAY THE SPEED REDUCTIONS ARE NEEDED TO REPAIR SOME DAMAGED TRACKBEDS.

THEY ESTIMATE THE SLOWER TRAINS WILL ONLY ADD 10 MINUTES TO THE COMMUTE.

Situation Notes for story B

CommuterRail train drivers will begin a job action slowdown on Monday because they have been working without a contract for the past 13 months. They will follow all safety rules and won't work overtime. Managers say this will cause the commute trains to run at least 30 minutes late and will inconvenience most commuters.

Write a segue lead sentence for story B. Try to keep it to 11 words.

....

....

....

....

Feature or Soft Leads

Many times you will work on a story that is timeless and can be banked for weeks without getting old. Often called an "evergreen" or an "H-F-R" (hold for release), this is the area of soft news—the human interest feature story. These stories don't have any immediacy angle, or reax, or perspective. In many cases, it will take a clever bit of writing to fashion the lead.

The lead for the feature story can often be found in the more universal themes it represents or in the commonsense lessons it provides. In unusual cases, you might have to resort to well-known quotations, sayings, metaphors, song lyrics, or poems.

Let's say this story involves a construction worker who has invented a special, money-saving drill for the new Steeltown sewer project. It's not a new story, or a reax, or a folo. There's not a lot of perspective to use. Certainly, there's no segue in sight.

The feature lead is what's left. Here, the writer is slowly backing into the story by highlighting the unusual nature of this event.

> A SEWER WORKER'S FRUSTRATION WITH THE SLOW PACE OF TUN-NELING WILL NOW SAVE STEELTOWN A BUNDLE OF MONEY.
> WELDER AURELIO CASTENAGA NEVER THOUGHT THE STANDARD ROOM-SIZED DRILL BITS WORKED EFFICIENTLY ON THE CARLSON STREET PROJECT.
> CASTENAGA . . .

It took almost 10 seconds before we got to the real drill invention story angle. This circuitous feature lead can get even more cumbersome when the text grows to unwieldy lengths. Sometimes the lead can take up more than half of the time allotted for the story.

A second danger of overheated feature leads is that the chosen metaphor, quotation, or joke may not fit the situation. Here's an example of that problem:

> THOMAS EDISON ONCE SAID INVENTORS ARE CRAZY PEOPLE . . . BENT ON SAVING THE WORLD BY TINKERING.
> AND THAT'S WHAT ONE SEWER WORKER HAS BEEN DOING LATELY . . . GOING CRAZY IN THE PIPELINES . . . BECAUSE HE DIDN'T HAVE A DURABLE BIT FOR HIS DRILL . . . etc.

You might even get a lawsuit out of that one. It also brings up the third danger of the feature lead—inaccuracy of the chosen quote, saying, or whatever is used. For instance, did Thomas Edison really say that? Look it up. Maybe you only half-remember the famous old saying. If you are wrong, there are hundreds of viewers out there who know exactly what old Edison said and they probably won't be timid about calling, e-mailing, or tweeting to let the staff know about the blunder.

▶ **EXERCISE 4-H**

Feature Leads

Review the situation notes and write two different 15-second feature leads for this story, one using an old saying or proverb and the other using a feature lead of your choice.

Situation Notes

Two men are attempting to break the tandem bicycle record across the United States. They will leave tomorrow from a downtown San Francisco park and head east to the boardwalk in Atlantic City, New Jersey. They are Michael Denton, 37, of Arlington, Virginia, and William Popper, 24, of Devonshire Springs, Maryland. Their goal is to raise money for the Advanced Adult Diabetes Fund. The attempt is unusual because Popper is blind. They will be followed by a van carrying spare parts and personal belongings. They expect the trip will take 18 days.

....

....

....

....

....

....

....

....

....

....

....

....

....

....

....

....

....

....

....

....

Four Leads to Avoid

Some leads are awkward. Although not grammatically wrong, they can put the newscaster in a difficult situation with long sentences, dull writing, or questionable emphasis on words. The four we will consider are the jammed, cliché, question, and quote leads. Because of their awkward natures, they should be used sparingly, if at all.

Avoid Jammed Leads

A jammed lead is similar to the newspaper inverted pyramid lead in which the writer attempts to tell the entire story in one sentence. In spoken news, it just doesn't work. Both the reader and the audience need the pauses provided by scripts designed for speech patterns.

The best method of fixing a jammed lead is to break it up into a number of sentences or to focus on some keywords in the story and try for a new story or perspective lead.

Here's a jammed lead:

> ON A VOTE OF FIVE-TO-TWO . . . COUNTY SUPERVISORS ARE PUT-TING ON HOLD TWO MULTI-MILLION DOLLAR LIGHT-RAIL PROJECTS UNTIL A SUPERVISORS COMMITTEE BEGINS TO INVESTIGATE THE CHARGES OF FRAUD . . . MISMANAGEMENT . . . AND POLITICAL FAVOR-ITISM IN THE AWARD OF THE LUCRATIVE CONTRACTS FOR THE WORK ON THE NEW RIGHTS-OF-WAY AND SWITCHING YARDS.

Here's the rewrite:

> COUNTY SUPERVISORS ARE PUTTING THE BRAKES ON TWO EXPEN-SIVE LIGHT RAIL PROJECTS.

► **EXERCISE 4-1**

Jammed Leads

Review the situation notes and write a short lead sentence for this story. If possible, keep the word count under 11.

Situation Notes

You're working for the 6 p.m. newscast. At three this afternoon, a runaway truck smashed into a house under construction on a hillside above an elementary school in the Walnut Vista section of your city. The truck tore the half-finished house from its foundation and the truck and house plunged into the schoolyard. The house was worth $480,000, the truck was worth $15,000, and the load of glass the truck was carrying was worth $20,000. Two teenagers were playing basketball in the otherwise empty schoolyard. They pulled the driver, Roger Barnes, 36, out of the cab. Barnes was later arrested by city police for drunken driving and taken to jail.

....

....

....

....

....

....

Avoid Cliché Leads

Although clichés provide quick leads, they should be avoided and an effort made to construct a more original opening.

The most stale cliché leads are the "good news/bad news" ones that seem to pop up in almost every newscast.

THERE'S GOOD NEWS FOR CAR BUYERS . . . etc.

or

BAD NEWS FOR TAXPAYERS. THE . . . etc.

or

THERE'S GOOD NEWS AND BAD NEWS FOR DOG LOVERS. THE . . . etc.

The difficulty with "good news/bad news" leads is overuse. Because different writers prepare a single broadcast, the "good news/bad news" leads can show up twice or three times in a newscast. When this happens, the leads lack punch. Also, a "good news" lead is a bit of editorializing on our part. Maybe it was good news for some, but it could have been bad news for others.

A second tired lead is what we call the "youra" sentence. It starts something like this:

> IF YOU'RE A FAN OF HIGH WIRE TRAPEZE . . . THEN YOU'LL LOVE THE NEW ROCKET CIRCUS SHOW THIS WEEK AT THE FAIRGROUNDS.

Here you might observe that you are turning away the 99 percent of the audience who couldn't care less about trapeze artistry. Once you lose this audience, they won't be around for the better stories that might come later.

Practice writing all of your stories without using "good news/bad news" or "youra" leads. The day will come when you are overloaded with work, the deadline is five minutes away, and your brain has ceased to function. That's the time to resurrect this tired old lead.

Avoid Rhetorical Question Leads

Rhetorical question leads are an old broadcast standby. They show up in many newscasts, more than they need to. As with cliché leads, the question format becomes stale after the second or third use. If you alone are writing and reading the newscast, there shouldn't be a problem. Otherwise, it would be best to skip these.

> WHAT DOES EVERYONE DOWN AT COUNTY JAIL WANT IN THE OLD CHRISTMAS STOCKING?
> WELL . . . IT COULD BE A GOOD PAIR OF EAR PLUGS . . . etc.

Or maybe a saw? Your question might be better off as a statement:

> THE SHERIFFS OFFICE SAYS THAT INMATES DOWN AT COUNTY JAIL HAVE BEEN ASKING FOR EARPLUGS.

There is something else to consider. Rhetorical questions are tough on the newscaster, especially if he or she gets the copy at the last minute or has to read the lead sentence cold. Sometimes it's hard to get the right inflection. Other times, the rhetorical question may simply allow the audience to answer "no" or "so what" and then ignore your story.

What if you are the newscaster? As you become more skilled and are writing for yourself, there's nothing wrong with an occasional rhetorical opening. You'll know it's coming and you can moderate your voice.

► **EXERCISE 4-J**

Turning Around the Rhetorical Question

Rewrite these rhetorical question leads:

WHO IS THE LUCKIEST POLITICIAN THIS YEAR?
    IT MIGHT HAVE BEEN BOB BOSTWICK . . . THE NEW STATE CONTROLLER.

....
....
....
....
....
....
....

WHAT'S THE MOST DANGEROUS INTERSECTION IN THE CITY? WELL . . . A NEW
STUDY SAYS IT'S THE CORNER OF B AND OAK STREETS.

....
....
....
....
....
....
....

Avoid Unattributed Quotes as Leads

Cold quotes, which are quotes without advance attribution, are tempting. They are dramatic. They sometimes stun the listeners and viewers. Sometimes, they even work: maybe once a month.

In the meantime, don't use quotes without attribution as leads. Otherwise you put your newscasters in jeopardy. Quotes need dramatic reading, and most newscasters are not ready to adopt a persona at the top of every story. In the next example, a quote without attribution led a story that followed a previous story about an unexpected tragedy. This was the quote lead:

I AM SADDENED . . . DISMAYED . . . AND SICKENED BY THIS WHOLE
MESS.
THOSE WERE THE WORDS TODAY OF . . . etc.

The newscaster didn't pause enough after the previous story, so it sounded like this quote belonged to the tragic story before it. The newscaster then became flustered during the remainder of the story. Before a quote, use attribution.

▶ **EXERCISE 4-K**

Comprehensive on Writing Leads (group)

Review the situation notes and write two lead sentences for this story. This exercise also can be shared by small groups, who would compete for the strongest lead sentences.

Situation Notes

This occurred at Hilltop Metropolitan hospital (the trauma center in your city) last night at 11:30 p.m. A neighborhood power failure had knocked out electricity to various parts of the hospital. Emergency generators kicked in everywhere except for one operating room, in which a Cesarean section birth was underway.

A quick-thinking nurse grabbed a flashlight from his backpack and held it for doctors while they continued the operation. The lights were restored in 10 minutes and everything went okay. Chief surgeon Dr. Mary Wentz said it certainly made for an interesting operation. The baby girl, named Luz (for light), is fine. Her mother, Maria Espinoza, 24, of your city, said she is thrilled by the nurse's quick thinking. The nurse, Byron Walcott, 28, of Fairview, said it was his camping flashlight and he was lucky he was just back from a trip. "When I turned it on," he said, "I hoped I had remembered to put in new batteries. It was weak, but by some miracle, it kept on long enough."

....
....
....
....
....
....
....

► **EXERCISE 4-L**

Comprehensive on Writing Lead Sentences

Review the situation notes and write two different leads for this story. This exercise also can be done by small groups competing for the strongest lead sentences.

Situation Notes

The school board met last night, and after a routine 12-hour session, they voted to close five elementary schools, all in the Riverview district, which has a high minority population. The board says the closures will save over $2,000,000 in the next three years. The students from the closed schools will be bused to schools in Manor Heights, which is a very rich suburb, with few minority residents.

At the meeting, parents from Riverview charged racism was involved in the reassignments. They pointed out that the schools were closed in their district because all of the school board members and the superintendent live in Manor Heights. You are unable to confirm whether or not that is true. However, you do learn it will cost over $1.5 million for the busing program in three years, an expense the district wouldn't have without the closures.

....

....

....

....

....

....

....

....

....

....

....

....

....

....

► **EXERCISE 4-M**

More Leads

Review the situation notes and write two different leads for this story. This exercise also can be done by small groups competing for the strongest lead sentences.

Situation Notes

Hundreds of shallow lead and zinc mines dug under Galena, Kansas, by prospectors in the late 1800s are collapsing and threatening to swallow aging buildings on Main Street, including banks, offices, stores, and City Hall. The ground is sagging as layers of rock flake off the old tunnels below. Now, the city is embarking on a multimillion-dollar effort to find and fill the web of mine tunnels that run beneath 60 percent of the town. It is estimated that this will take 15 years. Galena has a population of about 3,000—down from 30,000 when the mines were operating.

....

....

....

....

....

....

....

Chapter Summary

An engaging lead sentence should be a critical focus when writing a broadcast story. Merging the difficult job of attracting an audience while kicking off a narrative flow requires careful thought and repeated rewrites until it reads smoothly.

A writer can choose an impact lead that postpones story details or turn to commonly used models of breaking, folo, exception, update, perspective, or feature leads. Clichéd, jammed, rhetorical question, or unattributed quote leads should be avoided except under special circumstances.

5

Completing the Story Essentials

After crafting an engaging lead sentence, a writer must address the story's other crucial elements within the time restrictions. Although different topics suggest unique approaches, nearly every story needs a paragraph defining the scope or extent of the story's reach, a chronological narrative, story controversy or cause and effect, the "why or what" graph, and the future. This chapter explores some considerations when writing these story parts.

Glossary

PAYOFF A story written to delay a crucial element or explanation.

SCOPE A paragraph or sentence that explains the breadth of the story or how many persons or how large an area will be affected.

WHY OR WHAT GRAPH A paragraph or sentence that explains the change that is at the core of this story. It also may answer a question raised by the story.

Broadcast Stories Need Scope, Controversy or Cause and Effect, a What or Why Explanation, and a Future

A clever lead sentence may engage the audience but it will never carry a news story. The writer needs to concentrate on ensuring that other vital elements, such as scope and proximity, controversy and cause and effect, an explanation of central questions or the future are included. (See Figure 5.1.)

Scope

The story's scope is a single sentence that talks about the story's main theme's relevance to other story elements, population groups, or geography. This perspective helps the audience evaluate the story's proximity to them and the impact on their lives.

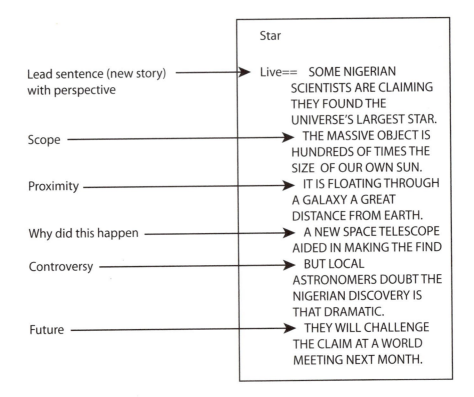

Lead sentence (new story) with perspective →

Scope →

Proximity →

Why did this happen →

Controversy →

Future →

Star

Live==   SOME NIGERIAN SCIENTISTS ARE CLAIMING THEY FOUND THE UNIVERSE'S LARGEST STAR. THE MASSIVE OBJECT IS HUNDREDS OF TIMES THE SIZE OF OUR OWN SUN. IT IS FLOATING THROUGH A GALAXY A GREAT DISTANCE FROM EARTH. A NEW SPACE TELESCOPE AIDED IN MAKING THE FIND BUT LOCAL ASTRONOMERS DOUBT THE NIGERIAN DISCOVERY IS THAT DRAMATIC. THEY WILL CHALLENGE THE CLAIM AT A WORLD MEETING NEXT MONTH.

Figure 5.1 Script showing elements needed for the body of the story

For instance, does the drug recall in today's story include a single brand or a family of drugs? Is the recalled drug among the medications viewers are taking? Did the chicken egg recall go nationwide? How many eggs are we talking about? Does a new tax law include low-income families? How big an area in a foreign country is affected by the flooding?

A single general statement can usually answer these questions and it can be covered in the second or third paragraph. Here are some examples. These come after the lead sentences:

THE CUTS WILL AFFECT ALMOST HALF OF THE WORKERS IN THE DEPARTMENT OF MOTOR VEHICLES.

THE OPENING OF THE SOLAR PANEL PLANT MAY MEAN 300 NEW JOBS IN THE TRI-COUNTY AREA.

THE HURRICANE IS HEADED FOR A 300-MILE STRETCH ALONG THE NORTH CAROLINA COASTAL ISLANDS.

FORECASTERS SAY THIS MAY BE THE HEAVIEST RAINFALL IN TEN YEARS TO HIT OUR AREA.

► **EXERCISE 5-A**

Compose a Scope Sentence

Read the situation and add your scope sentence for this story. It should follow the lead sentence already in place.

Situation Notes

Higher water temperatures this year are endangering the coral reefs in the Caribbean and the corals could start dying in the coming months, scientists said. The warning comes as the area enters the warmest months, so the problem is just starting, said C. Mark Eakin of the National Oceanic and Atmospheric Administration. When corals are exposed to warm water, they either expel or consume the colorful algae they host. If this process goes on too long, the coral host eventually dies. Five years ago, up to 90 percent of the corals in parts of the eastern Caribbean expelled the algae and over half died. This year, scientists are warning, the area affected could be much larger. They estimate that reef degradation would cause almost a trillion dollars in damage.

SCIENTISTS SAY WARM SEAWATER IS ENDANGERING THE CORAL REEFS IN THE CARIBBEAN.

(your scope sentence goes here)

....

....

....

Controversy and Cause and Effect

Despite the time constrictions in broadcast, any controversy mentioned in a story logically demands the writer must set out the competing positions. In many stories, it is more than easy to get one side. Often well-heeled or experienced interests will do a remarkable job of public relations while the other side is unavailable or lacks media savvy. So if a writer opens the door by bringing up the disagreement, he or she must be ready to explain this in concise and clear terms. Can this be done in one or two sentences in a 30-second story? Yes.

Often, one side in a public dispute is difficult to reach. Still, there is a responsibility to provide a balance to a story, even if it isn't on a second-for-second basis. If reaction to a charge is required and the writer can not reach one side, reporting the lack of a response fairly is crucial.

Caution is important. There is a difference between "NO COMMENT" and "WE COULD NOT REACH THEM FOR COMMENT." Each phrase carries baggage, and the more simple "NO COMMENT" might imply one side is hiding something. The more accurate phrase is simply, WE COULD NOT REACH SO-AND-SO OR THE OTHER SIDE (OR SIDES) FOR COMMENT.

A second lingering question in a story may come from a simple statement dropped innocently into the narrative. For instance, the story could say "THE POLICE LATER RELEASED THE SUSPECT." This might belong in our later discussion of the "why" or it could simply be asking for your diligence in completing the cause and effect. In this case, it might be, "POLICE LATER RELEASED THE SUSPECT ON BAIL."

► **EXERCISE 5-B**

Explain the Controversy and Indicate Response

Write a complete :30 reader that includes the controversy. Be sure to fairly report the response (or lack of it) to the charges made by the new organizers.

Situation Notes

A group of professional big wave ocean surfers have formed their own company and will take over hosting California's legendary Mavericks big-wave contest, known as the Super Bowl of surfing in Half Moon Bay, California. The previous organizers, Mavericks Surf Ventures, had run the worldwide contest since 2003. But now the local political entity, the San Mateo County supervisors, who control the permits for the contest, have approved the new alternative group. The new managers had argued that the previous organizers were slow to line up sponsors, slow to pay athletes, and failed to produce a highlight video. Calls to the current managers, the Maverick Surf Ventures group, only reached an answering machine.

....

....

....

....

....

....

....

....

....

The "Why" or "What" Graph

Stories often set up a question about an item's unique nature or central topic and then never get around to answering it. This is frustrating for the viewers. A writer needs to be certain that you are providing the answers. That's journalism. Here's an example of a script lacking the "why graph":

> A NEW CHARTER HIGH SCHOOL IN JACKSONVILLE IS COMPLETELY HIGH TECH.
>
> THE 65 STUDENTS AT THE FLEX STREET CAMPUS SHOW UP EACH DAY WITH A LAPTOP COMPUTER . . . AND COVER THE SAME RANGE OF CLASSES ONE WOULD FIND IN A TRADITIONAL SCHOOL. THERE ARE EVEN SPORTS TEAMS . . . SOCIAL ACTIVITIES AND SCHOOL DANCES.
>
> PUBLIC FUNDS PAY FOR THIS ALTERNATIVE EXPERIMENT . . . AND THE TEACHERS SAY IT IS WORKING.
>
> STUDENTS AT FLEX HIGH FINISHED IN THE TOP TEN PERCENT OF FLORIDA'S HIGH SCHOOL ENROLLMENT.

This highly compressed story is frustrating. Why is Flex High different? It leaves out the core element—that teachers do not stand in front of the classroom and the students take all their courses as self-paced instruction online. Here's the rewrite:

> A NEW CHARTER HIGH SCHOOL IN JACKSONVILLE IS COMPLETELY HIGH TECH.
>
> THE 65 STUDENTS AT THE FLEX STREET CAMPUS SHOW UP EACH DAY WITH A LAPTOP COMPUTER . . . BUT DO NOT SIT IN A CLASS-ROOM. THEY <u>TAKE ALL THEIR COURSES AT A SELF-PACED SPEED ON-LINE. TEACHERS ARE AVAILABLE FOR CONSULTATION.</u>
>
> THE CURRICULUM INCLUDES THE SAME RANGE OF CLASSES AS IN A TRADITIONAL SCHOOL AND THERE ARE EVEN SPORTS TEAMS AND SCHOOL DANCES.
>
> PUBLIC FUNDS PAY FOR THE EXPERIMENT . . . AND THE TEACHERS SAY IT IS WORKING.
>
> STUDENTS AT FLEX HIGH FINISHED IN THE TOP TEN PERCENT OF FLORIDA'S HIGH SCHOOL ENROLLMENT.

Finding the Missing Questions

This short business story leaves us with questions. What's missing? What questions pop into your mind when you hear this airline story? Write these down and add two or three important elements you would research and report to make the story complete.

> SOUTHWEST AIRLINES IS BUYING RIVAL LOW-COST AIRLINE AIR TRAN FOR OVER THREE BILLION DOLLARS.
>
> THE MERGER WILL FORM THE LARGEST LOW-COST AIRLINE IN THE UNITED STATES.

► **EXERCISE 5-D**

Including the Why or What

Read these situation notes. Now, make a list of at least three questions you might have. Finally, go online to the three-year study by the Dr. Robert C. and Veronica Atkins Center for Weight and Health at U.C. Berkeley to answer your questions. Then, write a :20 reader, making sure that you include enough details to answer the questions posed in the story.

Situation Notes

A new study by the University of California at Berkeley shows that a five-year-old plan to improve elementary and high school nutrition in Berkeley's city schools is working. The Berkeley program, inspired and guided by a local chef, combined classes in gardening, cooking, and nutrition with a total makeover of the school food served in the cafeteria. These classes began in elementary school and continued through middle school. Then a three-year study looked at the eating habits of the children in the program compared to other similar school districts. It found that the kids in the Berkeley district ate a more healthy diet, requesting vegetables and greens instead of fried foods. A majority of the parents agreed that the program had changed their kids' eating habits.

Including the Future

Spoken news stories that follow a conversational model usually end when the text describes what might happen next. The sentence explaining the future generally is placed last. Here's an example:

> HUNTINGTON BEACH POLICE SAY A TOTAL OF NINE BOYS ARE IN THE HOSPITAL AFTER EATING COOKIES THAT CONTAINED MARIJUANA.
>
> POLICE SAID THE LATEST VICTIM WAS AN 11-YEAR-OLD BROUGHT IN SATURDAY NIGHT FOR MARIJUANA POISONING. THE BOY HAD BEEN VOMITING AND COMPLAINING OF HEADACHES.
>
> EIGHT FRIENDS OF THE BOYS . . . AGES NINE AND TEN . . . ALSO WERE HOSPITALIZED.
>
> POLICE SAID THAT ONE OF THE BOYS PARENT HAD ACCEPTED THE COOKIES AS A GIFT FROM A NEIGHBOR . . . BUT DID NOT KNOW THEY CONTAINED MARIJUANA.
>
> OFFICIALS SAID THE BOYS ARE NOW IN GOOD CONDITION AND WILL REJOIN THEIR FAMILIES TOMORROW.

Payoffs

Classic narrative suspense patterns occasionally are useful for features and human-interest stories. A payoff model builds the sense of mystery and natural drama by releasing incomplete bits of information a little at a time, while alerting the audience that the important information will arrive later.

But beware! This melodramatic device skirts the edge of sensationalism and belongs in the area of local human interest. You walk a fine line when you boldly lead the audience on, more or less promising that the payoff is forthcoming. Producers should not include more than one of these stories in any newscast.

> IT WASN'T UNUSUAL THAT A POSTAL WORKER HAD A SIX-YEAR-OLD FOLLOW HIM AROUND WHILE DELIVERING THE MAIL.
>
> BUT THIS SIX-YEAR-OLD CRACKED A FEW SIDEWALKS IN THE FAIRVIEW NEIGHBORHOOD WHILE TAGGING AFTER CARRIER BOB JENKINS ON HIS ROUTE.
>
> WHILE BOB CAREFULLY PLACED THE LETTERS AND PACKAGES IN THE SLOTS . . . THE YOUNGSTER'S PRESENCE DELIGHTED THE NEIGHBORHOOD CHILDREN.
>
> BOB'S FRIEND ON THE ROUTE TODAY . . . A CIRCUS ELEPHANT NAMED ROXIE.
>
> ALL PART OF A PROMOTION FOR THE ROCKET CIRCUS DUE IN TOWN NEXT WEEK.

► **EXERCISE 5-E**

Writing a Payoff Story

Please use the payoff model to write a :30 reader. Save the information that the payoff was a lottery ticket and worth 12 million dollars for the end of the story. Begin your story with this sentence:

"AHMED LEWIS WAS ON A MISSION ..."

Situation Notes

State lottery winner Ahmed Lewis finally showed up today with the winning ticket. He had just 24-hours left until the deadline. The prize—$12.3 million, spread out in checks over 20 years. Lewis was a week late in claiming the prize. He said he had to retrace his route to Whitefish Lake, where he had spent a week with his family. He had to stop at each of the three motels where the family had stayed on the month-long vacation and check out the rooms and dressers.

   Finally, at his last one, the Lost Horizons motel in Bellevue, he found the ticket behind the nightstand. Lewis says his new fortune will allow him to quit his job and retire with his family to Florida.

....

....

....

....

....

....

....

....

....

....

....

....

► **EXERCISE 5-F**

Another Payoff Exercise

Please use the payoff model to write a :30 reader.

Situation Notes

A 26-year-old Brazilian chimpanzee named Jimmy loves to paint. He dips his brush in plastic paint containers every day for 30 minutes, and uses broad strokes to create pleasing canvases. Crowds at Rio's Niteroi Zoo love to watch the process. His trainer, Roched Seba, introduced him to the art because Jimmy didn't like playing with the same toys other chimps used. Jimmy's work is very popular with local art buyers and has been included in installations in higher end art galleries. Many buyers aren't aware of their artist's identity.

....

....

....

....

....

....

....

....

....

....

Chapter Summary

Every news story requires elements that go beyond a snappy lead sentence. These include the scope of the story, a description of the controversy or cause and effect, a sentence answering what or why questions, and an explanation of the future.

6

The Actuality: Gathering Useful Soundbites

The recorded field interview is a powerful tool for broadcast and Internet journalists. This actuality, when broken into cogent soundbites, can provide the credibility and emotion needed for stories that range from breaking news to human-interest features. This chapter explores the actuality's unique nature and outlines how a broadcast journalist can use careful planning to obtain effective soundbites.

Glossary

AMBIENT SOUND Recorded sound that is not part of an interview. It is also called NAT sound (for natural sound), wild sound, background, or BG sound.

BITE The recorded interview portion that has been pulled for use in a news story. Also called a cut or a sound pop.

TAG A portion of copy, usually short, that follows an actuality or soundbite and ends the story. Also called an out or outro.

WRITEUP The broadcast script sentence immediately preceding a bite. It is also called the lead-in, the intro, the throw line, the walk-up, the ramp-up, or the I.D.

Actualities/Soundbites

It is a broadcast journalist's job to interview subjects central to the news stories. These recorded field interviews are called actualities, whether they are on audio alone or on video. Reporters and writers select portions of the recorded field interview for soundbites to insert in stories.

Soundbites are used in the same manner as a print reporter's quotes. And although they are the interviewee's actual words, soundbites, like used car dealers, have a bad reputation. Critics often characterize them as shallow. With each political campaign, critics zero in on the "soundbite" as if they had discovered an evil secret.

When a soundbite is inserted into a story, the bite's visual and audio clues provide more than the simple spoken text. Viewers and listeners can glean as much from the speaker's vocal timbre, facial expressions, the body language, other gestures, or emotional delivery as they could from a simple spoken sentence. At times, these secondary subtexts provide critical information, occasionally contradicting the spoken text.

Whether or not to use a soundbite is a difficult decision; however, there is a good way to evaluate it. If the soundbite provides the viewer and/or listener with *more* than the newswriter could possibly craft into a script or if the interviewee emotionally tells why the operation is so valuable or explains the how and why of the story, then the bite is infinitely more powerful than the words you could compose and it must be used. But if the interviewee recites a laundry list of facts, mumbles or goes off topic, then you don't need the bite. You can write that information more concisely.

Interviewing to Get Results

When gathering material for a story, a broadcast journalist must constantly switch back and forth between two very different interview techniques: those done for **research** and those done to record usable actuality. The **research** interview is really a phone or in-person pre-interview that provides background for the story, collects data, and suggests topics for the recorded **broadcast** interview. It can be informal and can wander through many topics.

The **recorded broadcast** interview is different—it has a specific goal: to gather a full sentence answer from a primary source that is useful in a news story. Most actuality bites from these interviews will influence the construction of the story, from the lead to the tag.

Good actualities seldom just happen; they are the product of careful preparation. Securing a strong soundbite or actuality requires extra thought when planning the interview.

Select the Right Interviewee

An initial goal is to pick a good interviewee. Some subjects are much better at speaking to a microphone and camera than others. Some have electricity, life, cogent thoughts, and complete sentences. If you had your choice, you'd pick these over others. Documentary filmmakers spend months to find the right camera-friendly people, but in daily news work, you seldom have the opportunity to be choosey.

One consideration is whether or not these people are on the list of primary sources.

Eyewitnesses. Make every effort to find the authentic eyewitness and simply ask them to tell you what happened. Skip over someone who was told what happened. What is the better soundbite—a police officer telling us what someone else saw or the actual eyewitness?

Experts on the topic. You must be very careful that the expert you have chosen really knows today's story. Someone mildly interested in the topic may not justify the effort to get the interview. Even if the person holds a title such as professor of chemistry, they may not be familiar with the particular story you are working on. Too often, experts who know little provide soundbites for stories because they are the only ones available and the deadline is near.

Persons affected. Clearly, you'd like to be interviewing someone directly involved or affected by the story. These are easy to identify.

Test the Interviewee

Even if you have a deadline, you can rate potential interviewees during a research interview on the phone. Be vigilant if this person has no life in their voice and cannot complete a sentence without wandering off on a tangent. Do they mumble or have a heavy regional accent that might make any answer difficult to understand? If they do, you'll need questions that might keep their involvement short.

Ask the Right Questions

A reporter's goal is to have the interviewee respond in a manner that will give you short, effective soundbites. To insure this, the interviewer should recognize what question you want the interviewee to answer before the recorded portion starts. For the **broadcast** interview, you need to hone your skills at getting a short, cogent, complete sentence out of almost anyone on the other side of your microphone. To get that answer, you should follow simple rules:

- Don't ask rambling or multiple questions. The interviewee will only respond to one-half of the question.

- Don't ask "yes" or "no" questions. "Have you been effective as mayor" Answer "Yes." Because we won't be using the reporter's questions, the "yes" is not an effective soundbite. Instead you might say, "Can you tell us why you've been effective as mayor?" Now, suppose the "yes or no" question does slip out and the interviewee answers only "yes." You should be prepared to immediately say "Why?"

- Ask "how" or "why." These short questions will produce the most usable answers. But listen carefully to see that the interviewee responds with a complete sentence or isn't using jargon.

- Be prepared to ask a tough question. To get a response you might have to deflect the responsibility to someone else by saying, "Some people have said you aren't up to the job of being city manager. How do you respond to those charges?"

▶ **EXERCISE 6-A**

Formulate Questions That Result in Usable Bites

Review the situation notes. You are scheduled to interview Hidden Falls Councilman Trent Williams for a package. You are on a deadline and will have little time for the interview. Compose the three questions for which you want answers.

Situation Notes

Two 8-year-old boys were selling cupcakes in a Hidden Falls city park. They were trying to raise money for their neighborhood soccer team. Councilman Trent Williams approached them and asked to see their permit. When they admitted they didn't have one, he seized their stash of cupcakes and called the police. The police returned the cupcakes to the boys but told them to go home. Now the parents want the city council to bring up the matter at the next meeting and censure Williams for his action.

....

....

....

....

....

....

....

....

Pulling the Bites

Although a recorded broadcast interview is a lot of work, you cannot relax when it's over. Then it's time to start culling the stronger bites from the interview.

All reporters learn that short interviews have their virtue. When a deadline is close, experienced reporters know which crucial questions must be asked. If a recorded session goes on for 40 minutes, then the reporter has to listen to all 40 minutes to find what is needed. A carefully done 10-minute interview makes it easier to remember where a usable bite is buried and to extract that sound.

How Short a Bite?

The optimum length for a bite is always controversial in broadcast. Some radio stations won't use anything more than :10; the same goes for certain television operations. Others say anything up to :20 is permissible. Still others leave it open-ended, relying on the content.

Often it depends on the speaking voice of the interviewee, or how that person's voice rises and falls throughout the answer. Although you might need to shorten the bite for brevity, you don't want it to sound chopped off.

Many times this bite selection is done under intense deadline pressure. The reporter doesn't have time to listen to the entire interview but must go to a point where he or she remembers a good answer. The bite must be isolated, and the story quickly written, so it all goes on the air within minutes. For this reason, it helps to make notes on the location of good answers in the interview. Some TV reporters carry voice recorders with them and listen to the playback while returning to the station.

When deadlines aren't forcing the issue, and you have days to edit the story, it helps to make a transcript of the entire interview. You may find that the interviewee never really answered the questions. You also may find second and third answers that are revealing on other topics and themes. You may find a powerful answer that is not expected and that changes the story angle. Transcripts are, however, a luxury and seldom available.

Whittling Down the Bites

Because you can paraphrase portions of an answer and put that into the **writeup** (the sentence immediately before the bite), you can trim the bites down to usable size. The best place to start is to eliminate the parenthetical pauses, "uhmms," and false starts at the beginning of the sentence. In this example, the underlined portions are the ones you cut:

> Q: **Why are the critics after you?**
> A: <u>Well . . . Uhmm . . . That's a good question. I think they.</u> . . . . I think they are looking for a scapegoat because their convoluted and ill-conceived programs have all failed. And I'm it. Simple as the nose on your face . . . I've called their bluff. <u>They needed. . . . It's just like they didn't understand what I was doing.</u>

But if it still needs to be tighter, then trim from both the top and bottom. This requires more skill in the writeup . . . the sentence that prepares the audience for the upcoming sound bite.

> A: <u>I think they.</u> . . . they are looking for a scapegoat because their convoluted and ill-conceived programs have all failed. And I'm it. <u>Simple as the nose on your face . . . I called their bluff.</u>

▶ **EXERCISE 6-B**

Selecting Effective Bites

Review this transcript. Identify one weak bite and two strong bites, mark them, and read for time. Be prepared to defend your selections. This situation involves the extension of commercial zoning into what used to be residential neighborhoods.

Q: How long have you lived in the neighborhood?
A: 30 years.

Q: Are you upset with the council's move?
A: Yes

Q: Why?
A: You see . . . uh . . . my family has grown up and . . . uh. Well, the kids are gone now but my wife and I have lived in this neighborhood for almost 30 years. And it's been a nice place. And I don't see why they think that we should have commercial zoning, parking meters, and then, you know what's next, they'll be tearing down houses to put up stores. Look at these houses. People have put a lot of loving care into them. Families have grown up here. I don't know why we need more businesses in downtown Steeltown.

Q: I hear they're offering a lot of money for the homes?
A: My neighbors have been offered 20-thousand over the market price and I've even heard rumors that some have been offered 45-thousand over the current price. These homes are in the 250-thousand dollar range right now.

Q: Won't that help?
A: Well . . . that's what the business people of the city council think. Personally, they can take all that money and throw it in the river. This is my home. You notice they didn't vote to put businesses in their neighborhoods. It's just another case of the little guy getting shafted by the rich.

Q: You sound like you're ready to fight this?
A: We're getting a lawyer. We've already identified a few laws the council broke in this rezoning. We'll file appeals next Tuesday. We'll stall this in the courts. We'll take it to the Supreme Court if necessary.

Q: Thank you.

▶ **EXERCISE 6-C**

Selecting Effective Bites

Review this transcript. Identify one weak bite and two strong bites, mark them, and read for time. Be prepared to defend your selections. This interview is with Congresswoman Linda Belleweather, a three-term representative who is currently in a close election race that has featured mudslinging and serious negative advertising.

Q: Thank you for doing this interview.
A: You're more than welcome.

Q: Is the race tight?
A: The polls right now show that I'm ahead 54 percent to 46 percent. I'm sure I'm leading because of my votes supporting gun control and federal money for schools. The pro-gun forces are campaigning very hard against me and misrepresenting my stand on guns. I'm for a citizens' right to own hunting weapons but very strongly support strict registration of paramilitary weapons and battlefield gear.

Q: What have they said?
A: They say I favored taking guns away from citizens and my vote wasn't anything about that.

Q: Still you voted in favor of tighter gun registration laws at gun shows.
A: Yes I did and I would do it again. My friends who are peace officers asked me to stop hasty sales at the show. It seems our first responders constantly deal with powerful weapons traded at these shows. I believe in supporting the good judgment of the cops and sheriffs deputies in my district, no matter what other organizations have to say.

Q: Your opponent has also questioned your attendance at Congressional sessions.
A: My opponent doesn't know what he's talking about. When you are at work in Washington D.C., you have many committee meetings and many other commitments, including meetings with constituents every day. Often that means you can't attend every general session of Congress, but then no one does. My opponent is very naïve and if he knew anything about what goes on in Washington, he wouldn't make such outlandish charges.

Q: Some have said that you are running a negative campaign. How do you respond to that?
A: I didn't start with negative ads and didn't run them until my opponent launched a series of lies and half-truths about my record. Honestly, he just doesn't know anything about Washington politics and how it works . . . and he has no record of any public service to demonstrate his experience.

Special Ethical Considerations for Soundbites

The first questionable area is the context of bites. In print, interview quotes are often rebuilt from memory or scribbled notes. In broadcast, the answers are on audio or video recordings.

When cutting to reduce total story time, it is easy to strip the bites of their context by eliminating qualifying statements and preconditions. If these can't be returned to the story in the narration, then the soundbite might misrepresent the interviewee's intent. Here's an example taking this section from an interview:

> Q: "What is your thinking about the latest incident?
> A: I've fought against violence for 20 years but I can still recognize that someone will honestly say 'I think that violence in this case was necessary.'"

It is difficult to eliminate the first part of the answer and shorten the bite to the minimum. But if this cut is made, a completely different answer could be the result:

> A: "I think that violence in this case was necessary."

Second, answers should not be shuttled to complete another question. Maneuvering the questions and answers like freight cars could take them out of context. Although there is nothing wrong with using answers out of the original order, a problem might occur when the wrong question is linked to the wrong answer.

Third, avoid recording a better question after the interview. In radio this involves cutting in post-interview questions, and in television it means shooting reverse questions, done after the interview has ended and with the camera trained on the reporter. This technique is designed to help the reporter who stumbles through the question; however, it is hard to be accurate and usually results in a slightly different and more dramatic question. A better solution to a bad question is to paraphrase it in the writeup and only use the answer.

► **EXERCISE 6-D**

Doing a Well-Planned Five-Minute Interview

PART 1

This assignment involves field work.

Choose a story topic and angle involving a local controversy. Research the topic and sum up the problem in one paragraph.

Select a person to interview about the topic. Contact that person, do a pre-interview, and get permission for a recorded interview. Use any small recorder and microphone.

Write out the objectives for answers from the recorded interview. Write out the questions you hope will stimulate those answers. Make a photocopy of the paragraph, the objectives, and the questions and turn those in as Part 1 of the assignment.

PART 2

After Part 1 of this assignment is in the instructor's hands, conduct a 5-minute interview, sticking to that time limit. See if you can stimulate the answers you want. If the interviewee doesn't answer your questions, try repeating the questions.

Transcribe the interview. Explain if you got the usable answers you were seeking.

Chapter Summary

Broadcast reporters interview for research and for recorded actualities. From these interviews, they select short answers, segments called soundbites that are used in their field packages.

Soundbites are strong if they express emotion or carry a meaning that goes beyond simple data. Reporters can insure that they gather quality soundbites by paying attention to the wording of their questions and honing interview skills.

7

Using Soundbites From Those Interviews

The previous chapter explained tactics for gathering, selecting, and trimming down the most powerful soundbites. Chapter 7 focuses on using those soundbites in an effective manner.

Most bites pulled from interviews and then pasted into a story will influence the storytelling narrative. That means adding a soundbite to a finished reader will force you to redesign the story flow around the bite's content.

In this book, the sentence immediately before the bite is called the writeup. This writeup sentence eases the transition from a pure reader story to one with an actuality and provides the listener or viewer with an agenda for the bite.

Glossary

BACK-TO-BACK When soundbites from separate sources are edited together and are used without any narration track or writeup.

COLD WRITEUP When a soundbite is inserted into a story without any introduction or identification of the speaker.

Adding a Bite Is a Major Change

The decision to insert a soundbite into a news story forces a pivotal change in the structure. Because the soundbite's content affects the news angle and narrative flow, the story must be planned with the newly added soundbite's thrust in mind. Here's a situation that happens often in broadcast.

A common situation might go like this. A writer has already finished a human interest :30 reader on the new koalas at the zoo when the producer suggests that the writer add a :15 bite from a late interview with the zookeeper. The producer now is willing to expand the TST (total story time) to :40 to accommodate the actuality. Is this a simple job to insert the bite?

Not quite. The text of the bite is

"If that air conditioner isn't fixed, no one will be seeing any koalas. We'll have to send them right back where they came from."

So, let's start with the original story. Can you find a spot to insert the bite?

> A BIG CIVIC TURNOUT TODAY TO WELCOME TWO SMALL VISI-TORS TO STEELTOWN.
>
> THE MAYOR . . . FOUR CITY COUNCIL MEMBERS AND THE BEAGLE HIGH BAND WERE AT THE FENTON ZOO AT NOON TO GREET A PAIR OF AUSTRALIAN KOALA BEARS.
>
> THE RARE ANIMALS ARE ON LOAN FROM THE ZOO IN SYDNEY.
>
> THEY'LL BE HERE FOR SEVERAL MONTHS BUT IT'LL BE TWO WEEKS BEFORE THE PUBLIC CAN SEE THEM.
>
> IT TAKES THAT LONG FOR THE KOALAS TO GET COMFORTABLE WITH NEW CAGES.

Consider the new soundbite. It takes the story along a different path from the welcome for a new attraction and shifts the focus to malfunctioning equipment in the koala enclosure. The arrival of the koalas, treated lightly in the first copy story, now becomes a secondary angle in this more serious story with a soundbite.

To remedy the situation, you need more than a simple copyedit. You need

- a new lead sentence,

- a new body for the story,

- a writeup for the bite,

- a place for the bite,

- a better description of the controversy, and

- a suggestion of what might happen in the future.

The rewritten story will look like this:

> TWO LONG-AWAITED AUSTRALIAN VISITORS ARRIVED TODAY ONLY TO FIND THEIR ROOMS WEREN'T READY.
>
> THE RARE KOALA BEARS ARE IN STEELTOWN FOR A TWO-MONTH EXHIBIT AT THE FENTON ZOO.
>
> BUT THERE ARE PROBLEMS WITH THE SPECIAL ENCLOSURE PREPARED FOR THE POPULAR ANIMALS.
>
> ZOOKEEPER BRIAN ROSS SAYS EQUIPMENT BREAKDOWNS THREATEN THE EXHIBIT.

"If that air conditioner isn't fixed, no one will be seeing any koalas. We'll have to send them right back where they came from."

ZOO OFFICIALS ARE HOPING FOR A QUICK SOLUTION. THE KOALAS ARE SCHEDULED FOR A REST PERIOD BEFORE THE EXHIBIT OPENS IN TWO WEEKS.

As you can see, the writer must consider this soundbite when composing the story. Its presence requires new elements: a what or why paragraph, a time-consuming writeup to introduce who is talking, and a transition phrase to get us out of the actuality and back to the story.

Placement of the Bites Within Stories

Ideally, the bite should be placed in the story to allow a substantive portion before the actuality and a newscaster's tag after. In most cases, the portion before the bite is longer than the tag.

Opening cold with the bite is extremely difficult. An actuality dislocates the audience from the familiar voice of the newscaster. If the bite is too close to the top, it is hard to include sufficient perspective or compose enough attribution for the audience to make sense out of the change in voice or picture.

By the same token, ending on a bite can cause problems. Without a tag after the bite, you leave open the chance that the audience will not be able to separate this bite from the next story.

The Writeup

Writeup is the term this workbook uses for the sentence that introduces the bite. News organizations have different names for this vital sentence, calling it the intro, lead-in, wraparound, ramp-up, or whatever. Use what the local culture suggests. The rules for good writeups, however, stay the same, no matter what the terminology.

Rule 1. Keep the Interviewee's Identification (ID) Close to the Bite

In any situation, the name and title of the interviewee should come within :05 of the bite. In television, the identification can be dropped because the name and title will appear as lower-third text. But if that won't be happening, here is an example of the writeup identification used in television:

ZOOKEEPER LEONA WONG SAYS THAT IS NOT THE DIET KOALAS EAT.

"We have spent a lot of money to ship in tons of . . . (etc.)"

This next sentence is a traditional radio writeup. In radio, because there is no visually identifying graphic, the writer needs to position the identification as close to the bite as possible:

AND THAT IS NOT THE DIET KOALAS EAT . . . SAYS ZOOKEEPER LEONA WONG.

"We have spent a lot of money to ship in tons of . . . (etc.)"

Whereas the ID for single bites is easy, what happens with multiple bites edited back-to-back is a problem. In radio this is much more difficult and often precludes using the bites together, unless the voices have already been introduced, become commonly known, or are easily identified by gender. If both speakers are introduced, then be very straightforward in identifying who speaks first.

In some situations, no identification is used. This is known as a cold intro and it works only in a situation where it is clear who is speaking. Generally no identification is necessary when multiple interviews are done on the street with the general public or when the visuals in the video gives away the identification because of a uniform or name tag.

Rule 2. Use a Short, Complete General Statement

This is a chance to prepare your listeners and viewers for what is next and to help them understand why the bite is in the story. It is unwise, although it is often done, to leave a half-completed statement and allow the actuality to finish it. Your writeup (underlined) should be concise and set an agenda for actuality's content:

BUT GORDON SAYS THE KOALAS WON'T BE CHEAP TO KEEP. <u>EVERYTHING MUST BE IMPORTED</u>.

"We have spent a lot of money to ship in tons of . . . (etc.)"

This gives perspective to the bite. If well done, it also will help the viewer or listener adjust to the different voices and faces.

Rule 3. Avoid Repetition Between the Writeup and the First Sentence of the Bite

It is very easy to repeat words from the bite when you compose the writeup. If this repetition creeps in, it dulls the writeup's impact. The writeup will be stronger if the writer carefully avoids this repetition. In the first example, notice the repetition of the verb "brought in"

THE KOALAS WON'T BE CHEAP TO KEEP. SUPPLIES MUST BE <u>BROUGHT IN</u>.

"We have brought in tons of eucalyptus . . . (etc.)"

In this next example, notice how the writer has changed the writeup to avoid the repetition:

THE KOALAS WON'T BE CHEAP TO KEEP. SUPPLIES MUST BE IMPORTED.

"We have to bring in everything . . . tons of eucalyptus . . . (etc.)"

Rule 4. Avoid Throwaway Statements

A throwaway statement is an unneeded sentence or phrase that says nothing about the bite that is coming. Often, it praises your newsgathering efforts, such as "AS SHE EXPLAINED TO OUR CAMERAS." Avoid these. The example of a throwaway writeup is underlined:

AND AS ZOOKEEPER LEONA WONG SAYS . . . THE KOALAS WON'T BE CHEAP TO KEEP.
SHE DESCRIBED THE SITUATION THIS WAY.

"We have spent a lot of money to ship in tons of . . . (etc.)"

The throwaway sentence is worthless and if it is deleted, no important explanation is lost:

AND AS ZOOKEEPER LEONA WINGS SAYS . . . THE KOALAS WON'T BE CHEAP TO KEEP.

"We have spent a lot of money to ship in tons of . . . (etc.)"

► **EXERCISE 7-A**

Choose the Best Writeup

Examine the four numbered writeup sentences in this story. Evaluate each and select the one you think makes the best link between the first two sentences of the story text and the bite.

THE STATE IS STEPPING UP THE PRESSURE AGAINST DISHONEST USED CAR DEALERS.

TODAY THE LAWMAKERS PASSED THE LEMON BILL . . . REQUIRING A WINDOW STICKER ON ALL CARS.

(Possible writeups are listed. It will follow the preceding sentences. You pick the one that is the best.)

1. STATE CONSUMER AFFAIRS CHIEF SHARILEE WOOL SAYS SHE WILL NO LONGER FEEL SORRY FOR USED CAR BUYERS.

2. STATE CONSUMER AFFAIRS CHIEF SHARILEE WOOL SOME WON'T GO TO THE TROUBLE OF READING THE WINDOW STICKER.

3. STATE CONSUMER AFFAIRS CHIEF SHARILEE WOOL EXPLAINED IT THIS WAY TO US IN AN INTERVIEW WITH K-560 NEWS.

4. STATE CONSUMER AFFAIRS CHIEF SHARILEE WOOL SAYS THIS LONG-AWAITED LEGISLATION ONLY GOES SO FAR.

Bite:

"Although this has been a long-time coming and is a godsend, some still won't read the window sticker."

Getting Out of the Bite: The Tag

The text that follows the bite is called the tag. This is a good place for a number of items. First, put information here that didn't fit into the story before the bite. Second, the interviewee can be re-identified, something more useful in radio. Start the tag with the speaker's name. "CLARK ALSO SAID. . . ."

You can smooth the continuity into the tag by using repetition. Choose a keyword or phrase from the last sentence of the bite and repeat it in the first sentence of the text after the bite. In this example, it's "solving the parking mess."

Picking up in the middle of the bite:

". . . and I just don't see how this will help solve the parking mess."

BUT <u>SOLVING THE PARKING MESS</u> WASN'T THE ONLY PRIORITY FOR THE CITY'S TEAM.
THEY HAD TO . . . (etc.)

Writing the Story With a Soundbite

If you are setting out to write the story with a soundbite, the first step is to pull the bite. After that, consult with the producer for the story format. What's the TST? Will the anchor read only the studio intro or do you need a tag?

To try out this exercise, copy that bite into the middle of a blank page. By looking at the bite, you will be able to recognize what you need to do to get to the bite and how you will get out of it (see Figure 7.1).

Step 1 - Position the bite in the middle of a blank page.	**Step 2** - Write the story to fit the bite.
	O/C THE COLLEGE TRUSTEES VOTED TO RAISE TUITION AND FEES TEN PERCENT
	TRUSTEE SPOKESPERSON ANN DEVORE SAID THEY HAD NO CHOICE.
"We believe this is the best path to take at this time."	**"We believe this is the best path to take at this time."**
	O/C THE UNIVERSITY IS FACING A 300-MILLION DOLLAR BUDGET SHORTFALL.

Figure 7.1 The text on the left shows how you might position the bite's transcript in the middle of the page. On the right, the writer has begun to add the story text to flow into and out of the soundbite.

► **EXERCISE 7-B**

Using Bites

Select two concise bites from the following transcript. Position each in the middle of a blank page and on a separate page, write a story (about :30 total) around each of the bites. Be sure that the writeups conform to the rules.

Situation Notes

Your city has approved a three-block extension of commercial zoning into nearby residential neighborhoods. The council members believe that the blending of shops and homes will help the city's merchants battle the big chain retailers out by the freeway. There had been bitter opposition from the residents to the plan. The interview is with Bonny Frietas, a longtime resident and leader of the ad hoc group opposing the plan.

Q: How long have you lived in the neighborhood?
A: 30 years.

Q: Why are you upset with the council's move?
A: You see . . . uh . . . my family has grown up and . . . uh. Well, the kids are gone now but my wife and I have lived in this neighborhood for almost 30 years. And it's been a nice place. And I don't see why they think that we should have commercial zoning, parking meters, and then, you know what's next, they'll be tearing down houses to put up stores. Look at these houses. People have put a lot of loving care into them. Families have grown up here. I don't know why we need more businesses in downtown Steeltown.

Q: Will you sell your home?
A: I will if they're going to put a bank next door. I'd sell it in a minute. But where would I go?

Q: I hear they're going to offer a lot of money for the homes?
A: I heard that too.

Q: Won't that help?
A: Well . . . that's what the business people of the city council think. Personally, they can take all that money and throw it in the river. This is my home. You notice they didn't vote to put gas stations in their neighborhoods. It's just another case of the little guy getting screwed by the rich.

Q: You sound like you're ready to fight this?
A: We're getting a lawyer. We've already identified a few laws the council broke in this rezoning. We'll file appeals next Tuesday. We'll stall this in the courts. We'll take it to the Supreme Court if necessary.

Q: Thank you.

► **EXERCISE 7-C**

Using the Five-Minute Interview From Chapter 6

Return to the exercise in the last chapter where you recorded a five-minute interview and did a transcript. Take that transcript, pick three good soundbites, and on a separate page, write three :30 stories for the same item, placing one of those soundbites in each story.

Chapter Summary

Using soundbites changes the design and structure of a news story. Writers who must include a soundbite should design the story around its content. Writers should also be careful to follow the four simple rules of effective writeups: 1. Keep the ID close to the bite; 2. use a short, complete general statement; 3. avoid repetition; and 4. avoid throwaway statements.

8

Building Packages With Bites and Tracks

The reporter's self-contained package is the fundamental spoken news location story for radio, television, video, or the Internet. This chapter describes how to construct the package by mixing soundbites and tracks. Additional video considerations will be covered in chapters thirteen and fourteen.

Glossary

ALTERED CHRONOLOGY A narrative model that flows from the studio lead-in to the present time frame, then to the past, then to the controversy or points of story development, and ends with the future.

LEAD-IN Studio newscaster's scripted introduction to a field package narrated by another reporter.

MIC, MIKE Both are short for microphone.

PARTICULAR-TO-GENERAL A narrative model that flows from the studio lead-in to a particular case, then to the general trend, then to the evaluation or future, and may end up by returning to wrap up the elements of the initial particular case. It is also called personalization.

PACKAGE A field reporter's recorded story containing tracks and bites.

REMOTE A story done by the reporter live while on location. Often lacks actualities.

SOT Any recorded sound. It could be stored on a chip, tape or in a server. If it is sound from a field location, it can also be termed NAT or natural sound.

TRACK A portion of a reporter's narration for a field package. Tracks are usually scripted and can be prerecorded for insertion or spoken live into the package. A field package might contain many tracks, with each track separated by a SOT or a NAT SOT segment.

WRAP Another name for a package. Also called the wraparound, wrapper, takeout, insert, or package.

Composing Packages

Packages are standalone stories by reporters in the field. They combine ambient sound, interview bites, and a reporter's narrative tracks written later. Done well, they can be complete, satisfying, and engaging.

To assemble a package, the reporter selects soundbites and then checkerboards them with segments of recorded narration called tracks, pacing these carefully until the story is told within the time allotted. Except for Internet presentation, these stories are introduced in a newscaster lead-in.

Audio Only or Video Packages

Packages with audio alone (radio/Internet) or those with video (television/Internet) have much in common—the basic structure and the need for conversational writing. They differ in descriptive track narration and the writeup sentences that lead into the actualities.

For audio alone and or radio, there is a clear need for a concise description of the story's visual locations. In other words, a radio package might need to set the scene in a phrase or short sentence. In video, the carefully constructed visual narrative takes care of that.

Also for audio, the introduction of soundbites is handled differently. Because video can identify a speaker with a lower-third computer-generated (CG) title, it is unnecessary to do this in the track. In an audio package, this is done immediately before the bite.

Different News Situations Require Distinct Package Approaches

Journalists often are confronted with two differing coverage assignments—the breaking news event on deadline or the more relaxed feature. For breaking news, serious backgrounders, and folos to current news stories, the soundbites will drive the design of a simple radio or audio package. The tracks are more formal and often serve to bridge between and set agendas for the bites.

Features usually have a more relaxed deadline. For these, the reporter has additional creative leeway to write conversational tracks that can blend soundbites in to take advantage of an overall storytelling narrative. In the feature realm, the narrative flow is carried by the tracks and the soundbites might be shorter or less to the point.

The Function of a Good Lead-In

Almost every radio and television field report is preceded by a studio introduction, read by the newscaster, called a lead-in. If the lead-in is carefully written, it can both provide information and carry the audience to the opening of the field report.

A lead-in has several functions. It establishes a general perspective to the story and then narrows to show how this package will fit into that. In other words, it alludes to the story, but doesn't give out the details. If it summarized the story, why would the listeners or viewers wait for the field report? The lead-in also serves as a transition between the formal newscast and the field work by identifying the next voice as the reporter or as an interviewee's soundbite at the top of the package. The extent of identification varies with station news policy.

The lead-in can be a place to put crucial story information that might not fit in the field report. This could be a story update, which freshens the information. In a television report, the lead-in is also the place to put non-visual information that did not fit comfortably in the report.

In this sample lead-in, the first sentence offers a wide-ranging perspective. It casts a broad net for viewers who might be generally interested in the story. The second sentence, which includes the reporter's identifier, bridges from that overview to the details in Track 1:

> FOR CENTURIES ZOOS HAVE GIVEN CITY DWELLERS A QUICK LESSON IN EXOTIC WILD ANIMALS . . .
> BUT TODAY'S NEW ARRIVALS AT FENTON ZOO ARE HARDLY EXOTIC . . . AND AS MIRIAM MCKENNA REPORTS . . . THEY MIGHT BE CALLED CUDDLY.

Track 1

Today, zoo visitors got their first look at the brother-sister duo of giant pandas . . . on loan from the Washington Zoo."

Not all stories need to start with perspective and then narrow to the particular elements that lead to the story. For backgrounders, the lead-in would use a breaking news story with a similar theme and then segue to the field package with the reporter's ID. That's a common practice when stations have stories on the shelf, known as HFR (hold for release) or banked stories.

For features, the lead-in can be long, sweeping, highly stylized and use clever wordplay. It is less direct and tends more toward narrative storytelling.

Packages Based on Two Classic Models

The Altered Chronology Model

This usually involves the hard news or breaking categories. Here it becomes useful to take story elements out of their natural chronology. The altered time sequence of lead-in, present, past, controversy, and ending on the future provides a good model. Bites are kept short.

Here's an example:

1. Studio lead-in. Begins with perspective but shifts to set up the time of the report.

> THERE'S BEEN A TURNAROUND IN THE FORTUNES OF A LOCAL CHARITY.

REPORTER BOB WATSON SAYS THE NEW MOOD AT STEELTOWN FUND IS UPBEAT.

2. Wrap script.

Track 1

THERE WERE BIG SMILES TODAY AT THE STEELTOWN FUND OFFICES.

(Adds background and scope)

THE 1994 CORPORATE FUND DRIVE PICKED UP 31 MILLION IN PLEDGES . . . ALMOST DOUBLE LAST YEAR'S TOTAL.

(What or why)

THE STAFF REACHED THAT GOAL DESPITE THE SUMMER'S PROBLEMS . . . WITH A SPECIAL AUDIT AND CHARGES OF MISMANAGEMENT.

(Writeup)

EXECUTIVE DIRECTOR MARY WILLIAMS SAYS IT TOOK TIME TO OVERCOME THE PROBLEMS.

Soundbite 1

"We were pretty low six months ago, but we stayed focused on this year's goal and that helped. Now we've really had a successful year."

Track 2: Controversy

BUT SUCCESS THIS YEAR WON'T MAKE THE CONTROVERSY GO AWAY. THERE MAY BE OVER A MILLION DOLLARS MISSING . . . AND SHERIFF'S DETECTIVE MIKE STONE IS STILL INVESTIGATING.

Soundbite 2

"We've been working on this for six months and we should wrap it up next week."

Track 3: Future

SO WHILE THE STAFF AT THE STEELTOWN FUND WAITS FOR THE OTHER SHOE TO DROP . . . THEY CAN START HANDING OUT THE 31-MILLION IN AID. THAT SHOULD BEGIN IN THE NEXT TWO MONTHS.

FOR K-560 NEWS . . . THIS IS BOB WATSON AT THE STEELTOWN FUND OFFICES.

Particular-to-General Model

Personalizing stories provides another useful model, especially for backgrounders and features. Your package will begin with a particular case, then move to a general trend and finally return to the resolution of that particular case (if you know it). To use this model, take a story of general trends or widespread effects (for example, layoffs at a local plant) and find someone who is personally affected.

The lead-in is general but funnels the viewer interest directly to the individual's story. The reporter's first track starts with the focus on the individual. Then the story reverts back to the general trend, discusses any controversy and future, and may end with the final details on the individual's case.

This model has drawbacks, notably when the focus gets too wide or when the featured person is not representative of those affected by the situation.

Writers must avoid the temptation to use too many soundbites. Minimize the number of interviewees, the number of bites per interviewee, and the number of topics in the focus.

Here's an example of this particular-to-general model, also known as personalization. The lead-in begins with perspective but moves quickly to the person featured in the report:

Studio lead-in

THERE ARE RUMORS THE LOCAL THOMAS WINDOW FACTORY MAY CLOSE . . . AND AS BOB WATSON REPORTS . . . IF IT DOES . . . ONE WOMAN AND HER FAMILY WILL BE BIG LOSERS.

The first track begins by focusing on a factory worker:

Track 1

LISA PETERSEN HAS WORKED AT THE THOMAS WINDOW ASSEMBLY PLANT FOR THE PAST 14 YEARS.
SHE'S NOW A LINE MANAGER . . . AND AS A SINGLE PARENT . . . LISA PETERSEN SAYS HER PAYCHECK IS VITAL FOR HER FAMILY.

Soundbite 1

"We're about one week away from being flat broke."

Track 2

> BUT LISA HAS HEARD SHE'S ON THE LIST TO BE FIRED . . . AND SO ARE 18-HUNDRED OF HER CO-WORKERS.
>
> IT'S A LOSS THAT WILL BE DEVASTATING FOR THE INDUSTRIAL SECTION OF STEELTOWN. TWO OTHER PLANTS CLOSED WITHIN THE PAST YEAR.
>
> MAYOR CARLY ROGERS SAYS THIS LATEST SHUTDOWN WILL BE A SEVERE BLOW.

Soundbite 2

"This is going to devastate the city. We've been hit before, but this is a big one. The company had better help out."

Track 3

> COMPANY OFFICIALS AREN'T SAYING WHO WILL BE LET GO . . . EXCEPT TO SAY THERE WILL BE AN ANNOUNCEMENT FRIDAY.
>
> LISA PETERSEN ISN'T WAITING. SHE'S TAKEN SOME DAYS OFF AND IS OUT LOOKING FOR WORK. BOB WATSON FOR K-560 NEWS.

Writing the Tracks

Before You Start, Checkerboard the Bites You Have Chosen

In a breaking news package, the bites will be serious and need formal writeups that set agendas and blend them with the other story material. Your tracks will also be denser and contain explanatory data. To build a breaking news package, begin by pulling the SOT bites and laying them out on a page. Then you can begin to conceptualize how you will introduce the first bite and then segue from bite to bite.

If it's a feature package, pay more attention to the moods and flow of the bites. Your tracks will be shorter and often will be designed to showcase the soundbites.

Writing the First Track

Anyone writing wrap or package scripts should be aware of the importance of providing the correct amount of story background. If it wasn't in the lead-in, then it should be in the first track. Often, the first track is a bit longer than the others, but if details are needed to give the scope of the story, this is where they should go. It should be written to flow after the lead-in and should be kept short, :20 or so.

The Middle Tracks

Middle tracks are often useful as bridges from one soundbite to the next. It is always good to segue into the track with some slight repetition from the end of the previous bite.

Middle tracks set the pace for the package. The shorter they are, the faster the story moves. Some reporters prefer to restrict these interior tracks to one sentence.

Cold writeups—or no writeups—can be used in the middle tracks, especially if the speaker has appeared in an earlier bite.

The Last Track

The last track is traditionally the place reporters cache leftover information before spelling out the story's future path. But when setting out the next steps for this story, avoid clichés such as "ONLY TIME WILL TELL" and "WHO KNOWS WHAT WILL HAPPEN NEXT." As a knowledgeable reporter, you should have hard information about the next step. Then, tag out with your name and station.

▶ **EXERCISE 8-A**

Using the Altered Chronology Model

Write a :10 newscaster lead-in and a three-track reporter's narration for this situation. Structure the report around the Altered Chronology Model discussed in this section.

Situation Notes

The controversy goes back to a planning commission agreement to allow a fast food franchise to move into an old, ornate bank building. The hamburger chain was going to sell burgers and fries from the old tellers' windows. The fast food company spent nearly $2,000,000 converting the structure but a local neighborhood conservation group smelled a deal cooking and filed suit to stop the franchise. They want a local judge to order an environmental impact report and stop the conversion. Today, your reporter is at the courthouse and Judge Dale Hart hears the case.

The attorneys for the conservation group presented a petition signed by 80 percent of the 400 families in the neighborhood, asking that the planning commission action be reconsidered. The judge has promised to rule by next week. The spokesperson for the fast food chain told reporters that legally there is nothing the judge can do to stop the move, unless there was fraud by city officials.

Soundbite from hamburger company spokesperson Rhonda Biftek

"We followed all the rules and have all the permits. It's time to let us build."

Soundbite from neighborhood activist Mona Nimby

"No one knew anything about it until last week's meeting. There's been a coverup."

....

....

....

....

....

....

....

....

....

....

....

▶ **EXERCISE 8-B**

Writing a Particular-to-General Script

Write a :10 newscaster lead-in and a three-track reporter's narration for this situation. Structure the report around the particular-to-general model discussed in this section.

Situation Notes

The Consumer Product Safety Commission has ordered the recall of over 2 million home treadmill machines made by the El Molino Company of Mexico. The treadmills, which are used by fitness buffs, have a regulator that keeps the speed of the belt constant. But the federal officials say that on El Molino's Lightning model X200, the regulators were faulty and the motor can speed up the treadmill to 25 miles-an-hour and prevent the exerciser from stopping it.

Already, there have been over 100 reported injuries from the treadmills, many of them serious. El Molino says it will repair the faulty treadmills if people will bring them to its facility in Monterrey, Mexico.

Morris Crowder, a 37-year-old St. Louis attorney, bought one of the treadmills and used it for two months before the morning he went flying off and was thrown into the wall, breaking his leg.

Soundbite 1 from Crowder

"These are criminally dangerous and the company didn't test the regulators but instead bought them sight unseen from the surplus military market."

Soundbite 2: Marvin Tread, a dealer in El Molino treadmills.

"We are sorry that this happened and we are offering to replace anyone's faulty model."

Chapter Summary

Reporting and writing an audio package will reinforce the basics of field story design. These packages can be structured in many ways, but two common ones use the altered chronology and the particular-to-general models. Coordinating the studio lead-in with the first track and keeping the others tracks short are important concepts.

9

Writing to Stills and CGs

To work today in broadcast or Internet news, a journalist should have mastered some elements of screen design, documentary video, and the interplay of words and recorded video frames and images.

Video journalists and newswriters often reference static visuals and computer generated graphics that are added electronically to the visual portion of the newscast. This chapter explores how to write the text that is coordinated with those still visuals. These visuals include over the shoulder topic boxes, partial screen text (CGs), lower-third text, intertitles, and full-screen graphics, which consists of full-screen text over a background, freeze frames of video, maps, quotes, and illustrations.

Glossary

CG Computer-generated text made up of letters and numbers that either are superimposed over video, a still, or a colored background. Also called a super, key, subtitle, or lower-third.

COPY BLOCK In a television news script, the right half of the page that contains the words to be read by the newscaster. Newswriting systems convert this to the narrow copy stream needed for the teleprompter.

INTERTITLES Short text block centered over a full screen color background. Often used as a narrative device rather than a data display.

OTS For "over the shoulder." This refers to topic boxes keyed into the corner of the screen behind a news reader. These boxes are graphics and often have CG text to add information.

PRODUCTION CUES Script markings in the director's column of a script page that indicate places where there is a camera change or where to insert video or graphics.

REVEAL A sequence of CG text pages that, when changed in succession, gives the impression that lines of copy are being added one at a time.

TOPIC BOX Generic subject graphics usually placed electronically over the shoulder of the newscaster. These usually remain in view throughout the story.

Visuals as Tools

Writers use words, but television news writers combine words and visuals to tell stories.

Anytime a graphic appears on the screen, it is a disorienting change from what is already there. Newswriters, although not trained as graphic artists, must assist in the screen design and be aware of the graphic's duration and placement in a series of visuals.

Working with the computer graphics artists would be ideal; however, in many smaller news outlets, the writer must select the graphics. Here are a few suggestions when working with visuals.

Always Reference the Graphic

This means that the text, in some way, must relate to the change in visuals. This is vitally important in the switch from the news studio image to a full-screen visual.

Let the Visuals Tell Some of the Story

For this, the writer must be aware of the visual's power. Does the visual provide easily absorbed story information so that it will not have to be written into the copy? An example would be pictures of a crowd at a parade. The audience can see how extensive it is. The newswriter can provide other information in the text. It is a waste of time to add excessive narration to situations in which the visual and the ambient sound provide the details.

Also, the writer must be aware that a visual has such a powerful impact that it will absorb the viewer's full attention. In this case, very few in the audience will hear any text.

Explain Rather Than Describe the Graphic

The narration that accompanies the graphic should not describe the television screen but should talk about the situation or events the pictures represent.

Design the Graphic First, Then Write the Story

Graphics should not be added as afterthoughts. The writer must choose or select the graphic before writing the story around the graphic.

Designing an original graphic is easier with a staff computer artist. But the writer must be cautious that the graphic designer gets the right details. If the story is a plane crash, then be certain to tell the artist what kind of plane (airliner, commuter jet, or private plane) and some other details that might be important. Also tell the artist if a CG title will be on the screen with the visual. With this information, the visual will be spot on.

Figure 9.1 L, Figure 9.1 R OTS topic boxes for the same story but different newscasts. The OTS is keyed in on the left but appears in an OTS monitor on the right (courtesy KPIX).

Partial Screen Graphics

Partial screen graphics appear while the newscaster's face remains on the screen. The most common example is the OTS topic box in the corner of the screen. CGs, which include numbers and letters for identification and informational purposes, are also used concurrently. (See Figure 9.1 L and 9.1 R.)

OTS Topic Boxes

Over the shoulder (OTS) topic boxes are a common way to alert the audience to the general theme of the story. Often they are selected from an archival bank of previously used topic boxes. These should be carefully chosen. Improperly designed boxes may leave a wrong impression, no matter what the copy says. For example, if the story is a fire and the topic box incorrectly says "ARSON," viewers may be led to think the fire's cause is arson.

Although topic boxes are constructed and inserted in many ways, the most common is to pass it through a pre-set control room switcher effect that keys it into the picture or wall-mounted monitor along with a CG that fits this particular story. This allows great flexibility in using OTS topic boxes.

Crawls and Clamps

For some occasions, CGs are used to update additional stories while an anchor is reading another. This is done with the addition of CG bands across the bottom of the screen. If the text is moving, it is called a crawl. If the text is stationary, it is called a lower-third CG or a clamp. (See Figure 9.2.)

Full-Screen CGs

Full screen CGs are electrically generated numbers and words that are superimposed over video or still artwork to add information. They can provide identification, display

Figure 9.2 Partial CG crawl moves across the bottom of the screen while the anchor reads a story on utility meters indicated by the larger CG above it (courtesy KPIX).

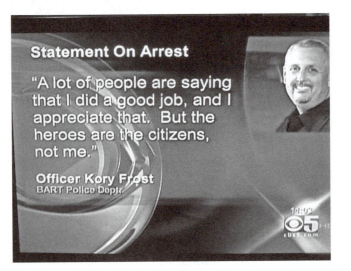

Figure 9.3 Full page CG statement by police officer is placed over the graphic and his picture is added in the upper right (courtesy KPIX).

complex data on a story, or show the transcript of a quote. Most full screen CGs are frozen, but if the text moves, it might be called a crawl.

How Long Should the CG Be On?

This has a lot to do with the image complexity, the text written to support it, and how the CG fits into the flow of other graphics.

A screen with words and numbers should be on long enough to read it aloud twice. That's the minimum. There is no set maximum, but you certainly don't want to leave something on the screen beyond the time that your narration has switched to another angle or topic. (See Figure 9.3.)

Figure 9.4 Full CG designed with title line and four subheads. This might be placed over a colored background.

Car Sales Up in June	
General Motors	9%
Ford	9%
Chrysler	7%
Volkswagen	4%

Using a CG to Display Facts

Generally, this full-screen graphic text is the responsibility of the writer. He or she must choose how much text to display, how long it will remain on the screen, and where it fits into the news story.

Here are some rules to help you design screens:

- No more than five horizontal lines of text. Otherwise, it gets too crowded and hard to read.

- Try to limit the letter count across the screen to 20. This will allow for a typeface that is large enough to read easily.

- The text on the screen should be able to stand alone. It should have a title that is concise but understandable. Sometimes it takes a great deal of effort to devise a good title.

- Know the capabilities of the computer graphics machines. Most can place bands of different colored backgrounds in the screen. Quite often, it helps to use one color background with the title and one with the information. It is also simple to color the letters, but you want to avoid too many colors in the makeup.

The process of building a screen is simple. (See Figure 9.4.)

Indicating CG Position in the Script

It is very important to add a production cue to tell the director exactly when you want the full CG to appear and when you want to return to the newscaster's face. It is the writer's responsibility to set the duration and this option should not be left to a harried studio director who might pop the graphic in and out when convenient. (See Figure 9.5.)

At the time that the middle of this story was read, the full CG was on the screen. Notice how the director and anchor both receive clear information about where the CG goes.

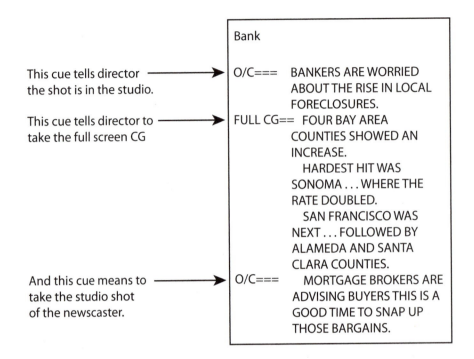

This cue tells director
the shot is in the studio.

This cue tells director to
take the full screen CG

And this cue means to
take the studio shot
of the newscaster.

Bank

O/C===   BANKERS ARE WORRIED
ABOUT THE RISE IN LOCAL
FORECLOSURES.

FULL CG==   FOUR BAY AREA
COUNTIES SHOWED AN
INCREASE.
HARDEST HIT WAS
SONOMA ... WHERE THE
RATE DOUBLED.
SAN FRANCISCO WAS
NEXT ... FOLLOWED BY
ALAMEDA AND SANTA
CLARA COUNTIES.

O/C===   MORTGAGE BROKERS ARE
ADVISING BUYERS THIS IS A
GOOD TIME TO SNAP UP
THOSE BARGAINS.

Figure 9.5 News script with full CG production cues to insert it and then to remove it.

▶ **EXERCISE 9-A**

Full-Screen Graphics

For this exercise, design one full CG graphic to present the data. Then write a :25 reader that opens in the studio and closes in the studio complete with the correct production cues indicating what part of the script is on camera and what part goes under the full CG.

Situation Notes

The federal government's Bureau of Labor Statistics has released a report showing the nation's inflation rate rose almost 2% last month.

The report also lists the Consumer Price Index results for different areas of the country, including (your city's) Metropolitan area.

In (your city), the CPI rose 1.2% last month and the price of food was up 2%, the price of gasoline and home heating oil was up 10-cents a gallon to $3.85, and the price of most new clothing was up $1/item. The cost of housing was up 6%.

....

....

....

Car Sales Up in June		Car Sales Up in June	
General Motors 9%		General Motors 9%	
		Ford. 9%	

Car Sales Up in June		Car Sales Up in June	
General Motors 9%		General Motors 9%	
Ford. 9%		Ford. 9%	
Chrysler 7%		Chrysler 7%	
		Volkswagen 4%	

Figure 9.6 The reveal's multiple screens. In this case, the lower right screen is designed first, then the subsequent screens are saved by removing one line at a time. In production, the reveal starts with the upper left screen and then plays until it reaches the lower right, giving the sudden appearance of a line.

The Reveal

The reveal is a very effective use of successive full-screen CGs. In this case, you design a foundation or base page and then progressive additions that, when played in rapid succession, make it seem that you are revealing information a line at a time. (See Figure 9.6.)

Using a Full Graphic or Animation for Illustration

Full graphics are most commonly used for diagrams illustrating a process or maps. In this case, the newswriter should sketch out a design for the artist and then meet with the artist before the story is written. If an animation is planned, the newswriter should suggest how the motion should look and let the artist handle the aesthetics of composition. On most occasions, the artist will offer advice about the design, simplifying it or changing its scale, which could affect the words chosen to accompany the graphic.

Simplicity is a key. Reduce the information in the graphic as much as possible, using only what is needed for the viewer to recognize the graphic quickly. The script instructions for this graphic are the same as for the full CG.

► **EXERCISE 9-B**

Design a Full-Page CG to Be Inserted Into This Story

Design a full-screen CG to go with this story. Write a :30 reader from this information. It would start on camera in the studio, go to the full CG you design, and then end in the studio.

Situation Notes

New surveys have found that Halloween is becoming a holiday where consumers are willing to spend large amounts of cash. In this state, it joins Christmas, Thanksgiving, and Mothers Day as lucrative holidays for merchants. The survey found that last year the average adult spent $65.82 per person on Halloween, up $6 from the year before. The largest spending category is for costumes, home decorations and candy, in that order. The total cashbox take for stores on Halloween is $1.82 billion, according to the market survey. And when it comes to costumes, pet wear seems to be a growing trend.

....

....

....

....

....

....

....

....

Chapter Summary

Switching from the straight-on shot of the anchor to a partial or full screen visual is disorienting for the viewer. Therefore, the writer must reference the visual, let the visual tell some of the story, and explain rather than describe what's on the screen.

There are both partial visuals, inserted beside, below, or across the newscaster, and full-screen visuals that replace the picture of the newscaster. There is also a composite visual that might combine a video freeze frame with a CG quote to add effect to the narrative.

Understanding Video Sequences

10

Writing text to accompany video has long been the work of broadcast news-writers, but in the past, they left the job of putting the video shots together to the editors. Now, advances in digital video storage and shrinking media revenues have made the editor position expendable.

From this point on, writers probably will be in charge of selecting material from raw field video. This means the video journalists need to learn the fundamentals for editing storytelling video and the basic logic of the video sequence.

Glossary

CLIP A single unedited video shot.

CONTINUITY The orderly flow of images for any location, action, or time period in a video sequence.

CU Close-up. This would be a person framed from the chest up.

ECU Extreme Close-up. Tight shot that frames a face from chin to forehead.

HIGH ANGLE/LOW ANGLE Shots in which the camera is moved above or below the eyeline to provide a different perspective.

JUMP CUT A sudden visual jerk in the image at the edit point of two shots that have very similar but not identical pictures. Two medium shots of the same subject might jump if taken from the same spot.

LS Long shot. A shot giving the sense of depth to a scene within the frame.

MS Medium shot. Two human figures framed from feet to top of the head.

NAT SOUND Ambient audio synced to the video. It can be used as part of the storytelling process.

POV Shot that provides viewers with a view as might be seen by a person involved in the action.

REAX Usually a CU, where the camera is turned on the face or faces of an event's onlookers.

REVERSE Usually a CU or MS, where the camera is turned to reveal the main event action.

VO Voice over. A television news story format that combines the studio anchor's audio with field visual sequences.

WS Wide shot. A shot to include as much territory as possible within the frame.

Video Sequences and Their Structures

Video that is used in Internet or broadcast journalism can range from a single running shot on YouTube to a complex, highly edited feature. The coordination between a clever and well-written news text and the video sequence is crucial to telling that story.

The video sequence is the basic building block for broadcast stories. The most popular sequences are short, from :15 to :20. A sequence assembles various shots to depict the continuity of a single event, location, or time period. In some circumstances, a sequence may be a single :20 shot with a lot of action or five carefully selected shots that last :10. Sequences remain interesting if the editor intercuts a varied assortment of WS, LS, MS, CU, and reverse shots; point-of-view shots; high-angle and low-angle shots; reaxes; shots with action in them; and shots with camera movement or lens movement (pans or tilts). Sometimes sequences are combined to form a multipart VO story called a wrap.

The sequence offers many advantages. From a production standpoint it can be edited quickly. Its pictures can tell a story without text. Its versatility allows an editor to compress or extend it to fit any time requirement. Done well, it can rivet an audience; but slapped together carelessly, it becomes a hack job of dysfunctional, confused clips that can befuddle an audience and dull exciting writing.

Journalists expecting to use video in their work need to understand the relationship of the shots and how years of editing film and video have produced a so-called grammar with rules.

In Figure 10.1, the basic elements of a speech to an audience are represented in the eight shots. An expanded collection from this event would include arrival shots, post-speech conversations, natural sound of applause, and many, perhaps 15, reax CUs of individual audience members watching the speaker.

The video doesn't stand alone; the audio component is also critical. All field video has ambient sound and it always should be mixed into the story. Certain shots also may have telling natural audio that is vital to the story. If the writer determines that the natural sound can carry and explain the news item, it might drive the story design.

Choosing the shots can be an overwhelming experience. Videographers in the field might return with 30 separate shots (clips) for an individual event, providing a writer/editor with hundreds of possible combinations to make up a :20 sequence. Finding the right narrative flow becomes a complex task. Which shot should you choose as an establisher—the vital intro to the sequence? Which clips will carry the narrative? How long should each clip be? What order should you give them? What compromises must be made so the final video story will fit the tight time frame available for Internet or broadcast work?

CU: Close-up from back of room.

MS: Medium shot from back of room.

EWS: Extreme wide shot from back.

WS: From side (reverse) showing audience.

MS: Medium shot of audience reaction.

ECU: Extreme close-up of anxious hands.

MS: Side of room with photographer.

CU: Side of room.

Figure 10.1 Examples of shots taken during a routine political speech by British Prime Minister David Cameron. Any of these selections can be shuffled and sequenced in a different order to depict the speech. Many more CUs of the audience would be available (freeze frame video courtesy of Ken Kobre).

Only after selecting the video should the writer compose a VO narrative coordinated with the video. If the video sequence is powerful in its own right, then the VO might not be needed. If it is weak, then the writer has a more difficult job.

Choosing the Most Powerful Video

Here's a generally accepted video quality priority list:

- The strongest possible video you can use is a well-shot and carefully edited **natural sound sequence**. These clips tell a story in pictures with natural ambient sync sound that explains the situation. There is often no need for VO narrative when the natural sound sequence is clear enough to provide details for the story.

- If the natural sound doesn't carry the narrative or isn't thought provoking, then a **sequence with voice over (VO) narration** would be your next choice. You continue to use the ambient sound with the video but carry it at a lower level while the VO narration becomes the prominent track.

- The next choice is called **B-roll**. Its designation is a holdover cinema term. In film work, the supporting pictures on the B-roll were sent to a lab to merge with audio and images on the principal reel called the A-roll. If the videographer has provided B-roll, it means he or she has given you particular shots that illustrate elements in the story. These shots do not form a sequence but show precisely what the story text will describe. If you mention boats, trains, and planes, the B-roll video will show exactly that.

  In the industry, B-roll is a term that has been co-opted to describe any video that is not an on-camera interview. For *Air Words,* we are using it in its more narrow definition as illustration.

- If your clips do not make a sequence or the B-roll is unavailable, then you must try for a **generic** story in which the finished video includes random shots related to this individual story but that cannot make up a sequence. If you must use a generic video story, you need strong, well-written VO narration to carry the story.

  An example might be a story on a decline in tourism to a nearby resort. To accompany the text, you assemble three shots including (a) a tourist bus pulling to the resort, (b) a guide explaining a local attraction to a tourist crowd at the resort, (c) and a family by the swimming pool at the resort. These are generic to the story but unconnected as storytellers.

- The least effective use of video is called **wallpaper**, which is a thoughtless collection of random but nonrelated, thematically similar shots. It is a lazy way out and the eventual story, however well written, is dysfunctional and can destroy the clarity of any script you write.

  For instance, in our story about the local resort, this wallpaper segment might have (a) a WS of the nearby mountain range, (b) pictures of kids at a nearby waterslide park, or (c) shot of tourists with guidebooks standing on a sidewalk.

The dysfunctional nature of these shots fights against any thoughtful, coherent VO narration you might write.

Some Imperatives for Sequences

As you can see, strong sequences are the most sought after field video. There are some general rules worth remembering when editing sequence shots.

- *Begin with the most engaging establishing shot (ES) you can find.* Most video news sequences are short, about 3 or 4 shots, and go by quickly. For that reason, choose your strongest shot to be a sequence opener. This establishing shot should either give perspective or should quickly identify the topic for viewers. Television's intimate screen has allowed MSs and CUs to work well as establishers. Relationship two-shots that feature two major elements of the story (for example, the trainer and the new seeing eye dog) are excellent as establishing shots.

- *Maintain continuity.* Continuity means the sequence is about one event, location, time frame, or activity. Most viewers can sense when your shots are out of chronological order or include multiple locations. A chronology example might be from a demonstration: the protesters gather, they confer, they march toward the police, the police prepare, the protesters push against the police, the police push back, and the protesters retreat. If the shots were out of chronological order, the story would lack continuity.

- *Alternate WS, MS, and CUs to provide variety. Alternate shots from different camera centerlines.* Two or three very similar medium shots or close-ups right after each other can be confusing. By varying these shots, you prevent the appearance of a shot that abruptly jumps to another moment with the same look (called a jump cut). Go back to examples in Figure 10.1 and you can see how the videographer moved around the periphery to shoot from the front, the side, and then the back for a reverse shot. You can vary the camera centerlines by moving the camera around during the event. The shots from different camera positions offer a wide-ranging perspective on the event.

- *Vary shot length.* A sequence that is a series of still :03 shots becomes very predictable. This can dull an exciting event. If the shot is easily recognizable—such as a sign or statue—then you might only need it for :01. If there are many elements in your WS, you might have to leave it on the screen for :05 if the viewer is to make sense of it.

- *Insert reaction and point-of-view reverse shots to help condense sequences.* A reaction shot is a CU of a face in the crowd, such as a concerned parent watching the rescue of a child, or in Figure 10.1, the MS of four audience members. After three shots showing someone at a podium, a POV (point-of-view) shot from behind the speaker reverses the direction to let the audience sample what the speaker is seeing. These shots are vital to editing. Encourage the shooter to provide these shots.

- *Avoid lifeless shots.* Video of a new building, for instance, is livelier if you use a shot with pedestrians in front of it. Video of the new hospice center rooms is uninteresting without anyone walking through the building. Choose shots with humans over inanimate objects.

- *Look for depth in shots.* Because the screen is two-dimensional, look for shots that emphasize depth within the frame. Usually, this is achieved by shooting events or scenes at an angle rather than straight on.

- *Never use the same shot twice.* Never!

Watch Out for Sensationalism

Sensationalism means different things to different people. It can be defined, however, as the repeated use of melodramatic visuals to thrill and amaze your audience. For any event, it is easy to pick out a sensational moment and highlight that, giving your viewers a misleading impression about events for the remainder of that day.

An example might occur during the coverage of a parade. For two or three hours, nothing much happens, except for the traditional flow of bands, floats, and reaction shots of the parade audience. Then someone chucks an empty bottle at a float and a scuffle breaks out when security guards wrestle with the bottle thrower. Back at the station, your producer gives you :30 total for the story and expects at least :20 of video. If you make the bottle incident the highlight, the sequence of shots necessary to explain it might take the entire :20. What do you do? Skip it and you have the predictable, non-exciting usual parade footage. Use it and leave the impression that the entire parade was a melee. Discuss this in class.

▶ **EXERCISE 10-A**

Choosing Shots for a VO Sequence

In this situation, you have 9 shots (see Figure 10.2) from which to make up a sequence for a :15 VO section of a :25 TST story (opens and closes in studio) about the annual Italian Street Painting festival in your town. (You can assume that each thumbnail is part of an exciting :10 shot.)

Situation Notes

Each year, the popular event provides entertainment and bands (you have good NAT sound) and serves barbecue. Part of Fourth Street in the downtown is closed off for two days as over 100 artists representing 20 organizations and schools use chalk to create intricate colorful landscapes or portraits. Cash prizes go to the winners. But on Tuesday, city crews will hose it down and the cars will be back on the asphalt.

Now, make a list of the shots beginning with the establisher. Explain why you chose this start to kick off the sequence. Indicate how long you intend to use each shot.

► EXERCISE 10-A *continued*

WS: Band reverse.   MCU of band (nat sound).   MS of poster.

CU: Reaction.   CU of painters.   WS of painters.

MS of painter.   WS of same painter.   EWS of street.

Figure 10.2 Nine freeze frames for video shots from a city street art festival.

Chapter Summary

A broadcast newswriter's assignment may now include the job of editing video on a server. For this work, he or she must need to be familiar with the logic of editing video sequences.

Writers should concentrate on selecting an engaging establishing shot; maintaining various continuities; alternating wide, medium, and close-up shots; varying shot length; inserting reaction and reverse shots; and avoiding lifeless and two-dimensional video. Writers must also pay attention to the quality of the field audio and whether or not it can carry a story.

11

Writing the VO Story to Accompany Video

The VO or voice over story is a broadcast news workhorse. In some commercial local newscasts, it might account for up to half the stories in a single newscast.

As stories go, the VO is brief, ranging from :20 to :40 of total story time. In the VO, the anchor reads the copy from the studio and video is inserted electronically over the anchor's face.

The writer must be aware of the sequence and continuity of video images and how to relate these images to the story in the most effective manner.

Glossary

CUE POINT A segment in the video where the continuity moves to another location, event, time, or action.

OFF THE TOP A VO story that opens with text being read over video pictures.

TRT The total running time.

The VO and Its Various Shapes and Sizes

Newscast producers love the VO. It not only allows them to condense video stories into a tight package, but it provides a method of switching cameras on the newscasters during the live newscast. VO writers must know in advance what format segments the producer is seeking.

Whereas the audio for the VO comes from the studio, the video and its natural sound can be inserted in a number of story positions. The classic VO starts live in the studio, switches to field video, and then closes with a live tag in the studio. However, the story could end while the viewer is watching video, or it could start in the video (off the top) and include a studio tag. (See Figure 11.1.)

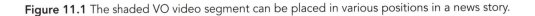

Live	There's a new duck at the zoo.	Live	There's a new duck at the zoo.	VO	There's a new duck at the zoo.	VO	There's a new duck at the zoo.
VO	The birds arrived today.	VO	The birds arrived today.		The birds arrived today.		The birds arrived today.
Live	The public can see them tomorrow.		The public can see them tomorrow.	Live	The public can see them tomorrow.		The public can see them tomorrow.

Live/video/Live   Live/video (ends)   Starts VO/ends live   All VO/no live studio

Figure 11.1 The shaded VO video segment can be placed in various positions in a news story.

Steps to the VO Story

Start by consulting with the producer about the story's news angle, the TST (total story time), and placement of the video within the story. These might appear in the story page block of the newscast computer rundown. Because the total story times of VOs may run up to :45, it is important to know how the newscast producer structures the item.

Next, the writer should screen the video and select the sequence or sequences. This selection should determine the exact length of each clip and their order within the story. The writer can then organize these shots together on the server or hand off the list to an editor to put it together. Cue points where the text must reference fresh video should be noted.

The newswriter should always choose the shots. Leaving this role to an editor could result in video that doesn't match your text. Or, it could result in bland wallpaper video that distracts from important information in the VO text.

With the visual sequence nailed down, the writer can then craft a clever, engaging lead sentence, whether it is a live studio read or is read over the VO.

Finally, write the VO text according to the shot design and length. If there is a topic or location change, then the script text must be that exact length. The writer must test this by reading it aloud and timing it, or by using the timing built into the newswriting software. If hitting a particular shot cue is vital, then the script text must be readjusted until the timing is perfect.

The Twin Streams Concept

The writer should design the VO as a dual story. Veteran television reporter and newswriter Bill Rukeyser used to teach interns and junior writers about the VO by having them imagine it as two information streams running at the same time, one the narration from the studio and the other the picture story that runs opposite it.

Both streams should be able to stand alone. If there is a production problem and the expected video is not inserted over the anchor's on-camera reading, then the story

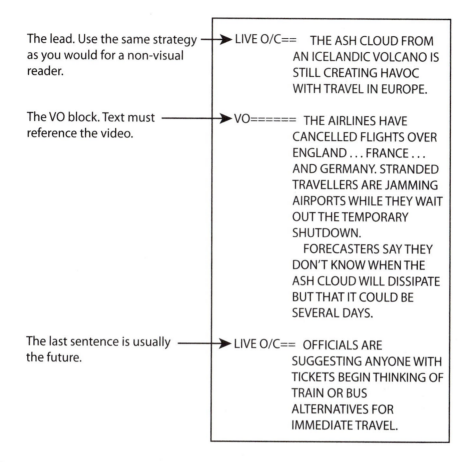

The lead. Use the same strategy as you would for a non-visual reader. → LIVE O/C==   THE ASH CLOUD FROM AN ICELANDIC VOLCANO IS STILL CREATING HAVOC WITH TRAVEL IN EUROPE.

The VO block. Text must reference the video. → VO======   THE AIRLINES HAVE CANCELLED FLIGHTS OVER ENGLAND . . . FRANCE . . . AND GERMANY. STRANDED TRAVELLERS ARE JAMMING AIRPORTS WHILE THEY WAIT OUT THE TEMPORARY SHUTDOWN.
FORECASTERS SAY THEY DON'T KNOW WHEN THE ASH CLOUD WILL DISSIPATE BUT THAT IT COULD BE SEVERAL DAYS.

The last sentence is usually the future. → LIVE O/C==   OFFICIALS ARE SUGGESTING ANYONE WITH TICKETS BEGIN THINKING OF TRAIN OR BUS ALTERNATIVES FOR IMMEDIATE TRAVEL.

Figure 11.2 VO story design as depicted on script page.

text still should make sense. By the same token, if for some rare reason the video appears without the audio, the sequence that the audience sees should make sense and contain many story elements.

Designing the VO

The VO design follows our normal narrative flow: a crisp lead sentence that engages, a text section that includes the scope and meat of the story while referencing the visuals, and a last sentence that provides the story future. (See Figure 11.2.)

Rules for Writing the VO Visuals

- *The producer sets the format but the video sequence forces the story design.* Newswriters should know that the producer will assign the format and TST, but the story's narrative text is based on the edited video. This practice only becomes a problem when there is too much information. A newswriter should be cautious not to overwrite the time set out by the producer or dictated by the video shots.

    There can be a problem of not having enough information. The assignment might be a :20 VO and there is little or nothing new to say about it. A writer will need extra research to flesh out sentences that approach the sequence's TRT.

- *Always reference the visual. Hit important cue points in the video.* For the viewer, each screen change from studio visuals to field video and back is a critical moment. Also, if there is a continuity shift within the video, say from a location to another location, then there will be a timed cue point that you need to hit. See Figure 11.2—where the text behind the video shifts from stranded passengers to the ash cloud. The writer should time the text so the reader is speaking about the ash cloud when the audience sees the video of it.

- *Let the visuals tell some of the story.* Look at the video without any narration. It should tell a story and pass along information. You don't need to write "TRAF-FIC WAS GRIDLOCKED" if the viewer can see it's heavy.

- *Use NAT sound throughout.* Sound must accompany the video in VOs. The ambient audio should be mixed under the reader's narration. And, if there is a unique NAT sound within the story, such as music, machine noise, singing, or perhaps animal sounds, then it could be noted for the director and a two-second pause inserted into the script. Often this NAT sound is up full for two seconds before the VO's narration begins.

- *Don't write text for video you don't have.* In the scripts that follow, which have a VO middle placement between a studio open and studio close, the first example uses general video of the fallen buildings and rubble to hit the cue point about the destruction. You can see how the words "A FEW BUILDINGS . . ." forms the reference for the pictures of fallen buildings.

LIVE OC===	ANOTHER DEADLY DISASTER IN THE MEDITER-RANEAN YESTERDAY.
VO ===	(vo) A FEW BUILDINGS ARE ALL THAT'S LEFT IN GRIMALDI . . . SARDINIA . . . AFTER A MAJOR EARTHQUAKE STRUCK THE FARMING CENTER. RESCUE CREWS ARE STILL HUNTING THROUGH COLLAPSED APARTMENT BUILDINGS AND STORES. OFFICIALS SAY MOST OF THE BUILDINGS FELL IN A PART OF TOWN BUILT OVER AN OLD LAKE BED.
LIVE OC===	(live) DOCTORS AT NEARBY MELEANIA HOSPITAL SAY THE DEATH TOLL IS NOW SEVEN. TODAY OFFICIALS APPEALED FOR MEDICINES AND BANDAGES . . . SAYING THE SUPPLY AT THE TOWN'S SMALL HOSPITAL IS RUNNING OUT.

What would happen if you had the same story information but only video of the hospital? Because video forces the writer's hand, the story must be redesigned. The script calls for the VO in the middle position, with the story beginning and ending in the studio. You'll have to change the script text to match the video you have and put the more general disaster information in the live on-camera reading area.

LIVE OC===   (live)
                  A FEW BUILDINGS ARE ALL THAT'S LEFT IN
                  GRIMALDI, SARDINIA, AFTER A MAJOR EARTH-
                  QUAKE HIT THE FARM CENTER ON MONDAY.
                    RESCUE CREWS ARE STILL SEARCHING
                  THROUGH FALLEN BUILDINGS AND STORES.

VO===   (vo)
                  DOCTORS AT NEARBY MELEANIA HOSPITAL SAY
                  THE DEATH TOLL IS NOW SEVEN.
                    TODAY OFFICIALS APPEALED FOR MEDICINES
                  AND BANDAGES . . . SAYING THE SUPPLY AT THE
                  TOWN'S SMALL HOSPITAL IS RUNNING OUT.

LIVE OC===   (live)
                  INTERNATIONAL RELIEF SUPPLIES HAVEN'T
                  REACHED THE DISASTER AREA YET . . . BECAUSE
                  THE QUAKE DESTROYED TOO MANY ROADS AND
                  BRIDGES.

All of this reinforces our rule: The video forces the story design.

Common Problems With the VO Story

Because the VO is such a versatile tool for producers and a common assignment for writers, it can be a victim of neglect and wind up with design and writing errors.

The most common blunder, in which the text doesn't match the visuals, is usually a result of deadline pressure or inattention to detail. For the audience, the upshot is a confusing story that leaves them in the dark.

For this reason, it is a good idea to follow our suggested routine when preparing a VO story. You screen the visuals, select the visuals, and then you will know exactly how much of the text is needed to explain the visuals in the story.

Writing VOs to Time

In this exercise, you must write a VO story that opens and closes in the studio. TST is :30. TRT of video is :20. The last shot in the video sequence must be the baseball bat. This will force you to hit a cue point deep within the text under the video.

Situation Notes

You have a story about eight large pieces of sculpture temporarily placed in four of Sausalito's city parks. These are cast bronze copies of statues by the French artist Auguste Rodin. Children are encouraged to climb and play on them. A community group called Art for People sponsored the installation. The sculptures will be in these parks for two weeks and then moved to another city. The Art for People officials think this interactive involvement will introduce the kids to the beauty of life size sculptures. But some critics are charging the statues will be vandalized.

Raw Video Shot List

00:00-00:10	WS of park with statues but no kids in shot
00:10-00:17	WS of park with some kids playing on statues
00:17-00:25	MS of kids climbing on sculpture
00:25-00:35	MS kids climb on standing man sculpture
00:35-00:40	CU of kids near head of statue
00:40-00:45	CU of kid sitting on knee of Thinker statue
00:45-00:55	CU of kid—head pops out behind statue
00:55-01:05	MS kid pounds a baseball bat on sculpture

Step 1 is to pick out the order of shots you will use and specify the length of each shot. The list must add up to :20.

Step 2 is to write the LIVE O/C lead sentence.

Step 3 is to write the VO portion and be sure you reference any topic cues you plan to hit. The VO segment must be :20.

Step 4 is to write the on/cam tag. Remember, this is where the future goes.

....

....

....

....

....

....

....

....

....

....

....

....

....

....

....

....

....

▶ **EXERCISE 11-B**

Adjusting the VO Text

This assignment is to rewrite a simple :30 VO script, which begins and ends in the studio, with :20 of video VO in the normal middle placement. The script that follows is the first attempt at the story, but it might be too long. You should read it against the clock to see if it hits the cue points for the video that are already edited and inflexible. If the text doesn't match, rewrite the script by removing words or phrases until the time matches the video cuts.

Here's the shot list you gave to the video editor:

00:00–00:03	Shot of pandas arriving in truck
00:03–00:08	Reaction shot of kids watching
00:08–00:14	Zoo workers lift cage down and open it
00:14–00:20	Zookeepers scratch pandas on head

LIVE O/C===	SOME PANDAS MADE AN EXCITING DEBUT TODAY AT THE LOCAL ZOO.
VO===	TWO SEMI TRUCKS BROUGHT THE CAGES WITH THE TINY BUT CHARMING CARGO. OFFICIALS SAID THE SPECIAL PRECAUTIONS ARE A SIGN OF HOW PRECIOUS THESE ANIMALS ARE.
	SCHOOLCHILDREN PUSHED CLOSER TO SEE THE TRAVEL WEARY ANIMALS WHO HAD COME FROM THE WASHINGTON ZOO.
	THESE GIANT PANDAS NORMALLY LIVE IN THE FORESTS OF WESTERN CHINA. THERE ARE ONLY 200 LEFT IN THE WILD AND ANOTHER 60 AT ZOOS AROUND THE PLANET. THE PANDAS LOOKED OUT OF PLACE IN THE CAGES.
	BUT AFTER A FEW MINUTES . . . AND A CHANCE TO ROAM THEIR NEW ENCLOSURES . . . IT WAS OBVIOUS THE ZOOKEEPERS WERE GOOD AT CALMING THE TRAVELERS.
LIVE O/C===	THE PANDAS ARE ON LOAN FOR TWO MORE YEARS.

Chapter Summary

Writing the text for a VO story requires great precision and attention to detail. Once the video sequences have been chosen, their times become inflexible. The newswriter must know the exact format, always reference the video cue points, allow the video to tell some of the story, use natural sound wisely, and avoid the temptation to write text for video that doesn't exist.

TV: Writing the VO/SOUND

12

The VO/SOUND or voice over into a video soundbite is a format routinely used in broadcast news. This style combines the VO, discussed in chapter 11, with a soundbite pulled from an interview. The writer must be aware of the sequence and continuity of video images and how to relate these images to the soundbite and studio on-camera portions of the story. The VO/SOUND format complicates the design of the script, making it complex to write.

Glossary

COVER (in video) Video that supports a certain amount of narration in a story. Used as a noun (Do we have enough cover?) or a verb (Cover that part of the narration.) When used introducing a soundbite, it often refers to production shots of the interviewee doing nonspecific daily tasks such as answering phones, walking, or conversing.

CUTAWAYS Short (:01 to :03) shots inserted into an interview sequence to draw the point of view away from the single close-up shot. Usually reverses or MS shots.

FEED Syndicated national electronic feeds of stories usable by a local station. These often are in VO or VO/SOUND formats

UPCUT An error in transition that happens when the end of the audio currently being played conflicts with the beginning of the audio from the next source.

VO/SOUND Also called VO/SOT or VO/POP where the "SOT" or "POP" refer to a soundbite. A commonly used television news format that combines a studio voice over segment with a soundbite. This can also be expanded to a VO/SOUND/VO or even a VO/SOUND/VO/SOUND/VO.

The VO/SOUND Format Is Complex

The combination of a voice over segment with a soundbite is a commonly used and difficult to write format for television news. Often, the VO/SOUND is extended to include another VO segment and is then called a VO/SOUND/VO.

Producers look to the VO/SOUND for many reasons. A reporter package from an earlier newscast may need an update and the reporter cannot be found. Your own reporter may be working on a package but didn't have time to get enough visuals or other interviews. You have a local interview but it needs to be combined with video from the feed or from archival file tape. You are drastically re-editing a network broadcast or feed story and you cannot use the reporter's voice track. Or, sometimes your station photographers shoot a story alone, without a reporter, and the story is handed over to a writer.

This VO/SOUND is intricate and must be carefully structured because its time restrictions provide little room for expansive writing. It is also the story format that is most likely to have production mishaps during a live newscast.

The difficulties with the VO/SOUND lie within its nature as a compromise between the VO—which can be done smoothly in the studio—and a simple SOUNDBITE, which is more easily handled in a reporter package.

A newscaster or live remote reporter generally reads the VO/SOUND. Total story time (TST) for a VO/SOUND might run anywhere from :40 to 1:15, sufficient for a good VO but sometimes not enough to combine the VO, the background that goes with the soundbite, and other non-visual information in the story.

Time is not the only problem. Both the VO portion and the soundbite usually are strong enough to dictate their own story design—but attempting to bind the two together may fail if they are focused on different topic areas.

Also, the soundbite may need :06 to :10 of a writeup sentence, and this writeup will need to be accompanied by video cover or cutaways at the end of the VO segment. (See Figure 12.1.)

The VO/SOUND Can Be a Production Nightmare

Historically, the VO and the soundbite were edited together onto one continuous source, causing problems if the anchor read too quickly (long silent gap) or too slowly (upcut and jumbled with the bite). This problem was most severe if the VO portion was long—more than :20. Now VO/SOUND stories are generally inserted over the studio video and audio from two separate sources, allowing the soundbite to be started at whatever point the newscaster finishes the VO text.

Designing the VO/SOUND Story

Any VO/SOUND piece done in a live broadcast must be carefully prepared and checked. Producers generally begin with some studio anchor reading and then go to the VO and then the soundbite.

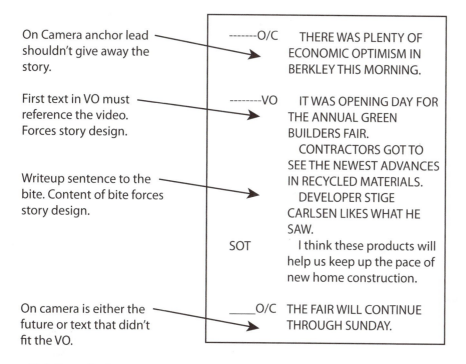

On Camera anchor lead shouldn't give away the story.

--------O/C   THERE WAS PLENTY OF ECONOMIC OPTIMISM IN BERKLEY THIS MORNING.

First text in VO must reference the video. Forces story design.

--------VO   IT WAS OPENING DAY FOR THE ANNUAL GREEN BUILDERS FAIR. CONTRACTORS GOT TO SEE THE NEWEST ADVANCES IN RECYCLED MATERIALS. DEVELOPER STIGE CARLSEN LIKES WHAT HE SAW.

Writeup sentence to the bite. Content of bite forces story design.

SOT   I think these products will help us keep up the pace of new home construction.

On camera is either the future or text that didn't fit the VO.

_____O/C   THE FAIR WILL CONTINUE THROUGH SUNDAY.

Figure 12.1 Example showing segments of the VO/Sound format script.

VO/SOUND Scripts Need a Strong Writeup Sentence and Visual Cover

Because the selected soundbite is now critical to the story, a writer must carefully set the agenda for it. This may mean transitioning from the topic covered in the VO to the topic of the soundbite. And the writer must then add :05 of video to cover that writeup, usually a CU or MS cutaway of the speaker at exactly the same moment you mention the speaker's name in the VO.

Use Another VO or an On-Camera Tag

Often the VO/SOUND format is extended by adding a trailing VO, creating a VO/SOUND/VO format. This greatly helps the writer, who can put additional information into the second VO portion. If the same anchor reads the next story, it's quite possible you won't need an on-camera tag.

Any tag, whether in VO or not, completes the story. The soundbite may be incomplete in telling the story and needs some perspective. The tag is also a place to paraphrase other comments from the interview that bear on the story.

Steps to the VO/SOUND

1. Check with the producer for the story format. He or she will specify the needs, including the time for the on camera portion and the expected TST. Ask if it needs a studio tag or simply ends in the video.

2. Review the field video. Pull the soundbite, keeping it shorter than :20.

3. Place the soundbite in the middle of a blank page. Think carefully about whether it needs a writeup, or perhaps it can stand on its own.

4. Compose the writeup sentence. Do you have any cover video for this?

5. Select the VO sequences you need. You'll probably have room for about :20 including whatever video you are using for the writeup.

6. Now write the studio portion and then the VO segment, being careful to hit any necessary cue points in the VO.

7. Read it for length and adjust.

► **EXERCISE 12-A**

Writing a VO/SOUND

For this exercise, write a VO/SOUND/VO script that is :50 TST, including :10 of studio on-camera at the top and a :05 on-camera tag. In addition, you must select which shots you want put together to make up the :35 of video. You have VO from different sources.

Situation Notes

The state highway department has announced it is going to rip up two miles of the Crosstown Highway and be working on it for four weeks to repair certain bridges. They will detour traffic onto another road over a mile away. Merchants who own stores on the Crosstown Highway are furious. The construction will limit auto parking and pedestrian access to their businesses. They are hinting at a lawsuit to stop the repair work.

You have :30 of file VO from an accident last November that was caused by a crack in a bridge on the Crosstown Highway. Several people were injured.

:06	WS of accident scene
:02	CU of Crosstown highway sign.
:14	MS of a victim on stretcher being put into ambulance.
:08	MS of tow truck driving off with one of the wrecks.

You also have :30 of new video shot today by your crew.

:18	WS (3) of traffic on Crosstown Highway.
:04	MS of exterior of Bob's Garden supply.
:04	MS of the Bath Boutique.
:04	MS of Glidden's Shell Station.

And you have an interview with Robert Gelden, owner of Bob's Garden Supply. Plus, you have these cutaway interview shots.

:04	Two-shot that includes reporter and Gelden.
:08	MS of Gelden only (he's listening to question).
:04	CU of Gelden only (he's listening to question)/

The boldface copy is the soundbite from the interview. It runs :14.

"Closing this road down makes no sense. How are we supposed to make money? With a little planning, they could only shut down one lane. This is the easy way out."

....

....

....

....

....

....

....

....

....

....

....

....

▶ **EXERCISE 12-B**

Breaking Down a Package to Write a VO/SOUND

For this exercise, write a VO/SOUND/VO script that is 1:05 TST, including :10 of studio on-camera at the top and a :05 on-camera tag. To do this, you must rework this package script on the donation of a $35,000 truck to the local county food bank. Remember to consider which video fits to run with which text.

Situation Notes

This is the transcript of the tracks and bites from the package.

(Shots of truck pulling up to back of restaurant and workers help load boxes of produce and cans onto the truck.)

Track 1

"The new refrigerated truck made its first rounds today . . . picking up excess food from 12 restaurants. The truck's driver . . . Henry Williams . . . thinks the new storage will help the county's homeless."

Bite 1

"We used to have to get this stuff to storage as soon as possible. Now we can go from source to source without the food spoiling . . . and this shortens our pickup times."

(Shots of Williams in the cab, driving to warehouse, workers unloading the truck, a forklift, and workers sorting the contents into large blue plastic bins.)

Track 2

"Shortening the pickup time is a big step for Williams. By keeping the truck on the route, he gets the food back to the county food warehouse in the industrial park in one trip. The day's harvest is sorted, repackaged, and sent to the six county soup kitchens. County food bank director Ellen Stephens thinks this will improve the food quality."

Bite 2

"It can't help but taste better because it's fresher. Before the truck . . . we used to have to store it overnight and send it out the next day. Now it gets in and out in one day."

(Shots of the truck pulling up and a worker unloading boxes off the truck.)

▶ **EXERCISE 12-B** *continued*

Track 3

Workers at the Rogers Relief Fund kitchen think that the quick turnaround is wonderful. As they unloaded today's supplies . . . they praised the fundraising efforts to get the truck.

Bite 3

"It took a lot of work. The people behind this idea spent days and weeks hitting up people for help."
    (Shots of the food line at the soup kitchen)

Track 4

"And those days paid off when the Freminger Bolt Company donated the last ten thousand dollars needed to get the truck. That was last month . . . and who was on the line at Rogers today serving up food . . . Freminger's president Bill Frannich."

Bite 4

"We're only happy we can help out. We know how tough it is in these times . . . and this is our contribution to the county."
    (Shots of truck pulling away from loading dock and then on the road.)

Track 5

"Truck driver Henry Williams was delighted as he made his last drop-off about 5 p.m. and then took the new truck back to the garage. The truck will be in use five days each week for the next four months . . . and then the food bank directors will see if they want to buy a second one. This is Ben Briley reporting."

....
....
....
....
....
....
....
....
....
....

Chapter Summary

The VO/SOUND is the most complex and time-restricted broadcast news format. It weaves together three forces that demand consideration—the original angle of the story, the influence of the VO video, and the implications of the soundbite. Combining these into a single story under a restricted TST requires very careful writing.

13

Breaking News and Feature Video Packages

This chapter addresses the field package—the bread and butter of a reporter's job. The package style could range from the simplicity of a breaking news event to a personality profile; a thoughtfully researched backgrounder on topic areas such as health, the arts, science, education, or community news; or a lyric and engaging human interest feature on the challenges or pitfalls in daily life.

Glossary

BRIDGE Any transitional narration (track) between two soundbites. Might also be a mid-package standup on camera.

STANDUP The reporter on camera in the field. A standup can be used at the opening of a package, a mid-story transition, or as a summation and description of the future.

TAG OUT The reporter's sign-off giving his or her name, the location, and the channel, station, or online site.

The Most Commonly Used News Packages

The reporter's short field package (1:30 to 3:00 TST), in all its variations, has been refined over the years in broadcast or video online news. It combines the credibility of on-site reporting along with artfully edited actualities to provide a memorable story for the viewer. It comes in many forms, including the more abrupt breaking news package, the perspective-laden backgrounder, or the light feature.

Comparing the Breaking News Video Package to the Feature

Hard news is the daily coverage of crime, government, business, marches, speeches, the courts, confrontations, education, and social activity in expected and unexpected events. In most hard news coverage, reporters and shooters play it safe by gathering sufficient sequence building blocks: lots of WSs, MSs, and CUs; cover shots; standup closes and bridges; and interviews. Each knows the structure for the hard news package is formulaic and may be a simple assembly of pieces driven by a straightforward narrative defined by significant bites. These reports usually are completed under extreme deadline pressure.

For these hard news packages, the crew may have limited opportunities for striking video—only one or two locations and repetitive sequences. Breaking news packages are more often built around the information flow in the audio track, meaning that the sound channels of reporter's tracks, soundbites, and standups can be patched together to carry the sense of the story. Often in hard news, the video is laid in last, edited mechanically to the rhythms and flows of the reporter's voice.

The feature story, on the other hand, often has a leisurely deadline. Reporters concentrate more on engaging the audience with powerful sequences. Feature stories, especially profiles, are pegged to the characters involved and the tracks can be more informal and lyrical. Soundbites in features are also trimmed more carefully.

Steps to Building a Package

Shoot for the Story Angle

Planning for your story's structure begins with the assignment. When you get the story, discuss the angle with the desk or producers. This conversation will tell you where you might want to start gathering your material.

Also, you want to consider a checklist of needs:

- Describe what video you will use to set up the present situation.

- Who is the key must-have interviewee?

- Who will explain the challenges or conflicts . . . and will this be in a track?

- How will you get something to explain the Future? Will it be visual?

▶ **EXERCISE 13-A**

Planning Ahead (Can be group project)

Pick a story from the news budget provided here. Discuss what you might find at the location and what type of interviews you might pursue.

Daily News Budget

FESTIVAL/ENDS 50-year-old Burlingame holiday craft fair is calling it quits after this year. Organizer says people aren't interested anymore in homemade presents.

SKINNYHOUSE Old Antioch house that is only 8-foot wide is on the market. Owner is available to give tour to anyone interested. Price is $450K.

SHARKTEEN A 17-year-old Bolinas surfer goes back into the water after a year in rehab for a shark attack.

TOOTHMOBILE A mobile dentist's office will be at Glide Memorial Church in San Francisco for three weekends to offer free dental care to those who need it.

COMPOST City of Oakland gets huge grant to start composting home vegetable garbage. They have a demonstration project going in one neighborhood.

SPACE VIGIL High school science students and their teachers are camping out tonight on a lawn at NASA Ames research center in Mountain View to witness a remote spacecraft's landing on the Martian moon Phobos.

....

....

....

....

....

....

....

....

....

....

....

....

Location

At the location, divide your time by gathering sequences and nailing down significant interviews. Do standups last.

Get at least three discrete sequences, as well as cover for interviewees. Don't make final judgments in the field about which sequence is the best. Later you could change your mind about which is the most engaging and move that up to the top of the story.

Other than a warm-up question, field interviews <u>are not chat</u> sessions. Control the interview by asking useful and strategic questions. Here some simple rules:

- Ask HOW and WHY questions.

- Listen. If the answer is not complete, then re-ask the question.

- Stay away from data questions unless you are looking to define the scope of the story.

- Don't leave the location until you have the requisite bites to set the scope of the story, describe the responses to the challenges or controversies, and/or talk about the future.

- Finally, when in the field, don't forget alternative visuals (archive, stills, graphics).

Archival stills and memorabilia can be shot onto video on location. Archival video from your library is useful, but is very often stale because news producers use it again and again for VOs and VO/SOUNDs.

Standups

On-camera standups are controversial parts of these packages. Some news agencies mandate that standups appear in packages as a means of enhancing the para-social relationships with the audience. But the deadline pressures of breaking news can force reporters to make standups as simple as possible and generic to the topic. By the time crews return to the station, standups done on location often are out of date.

Reporters have three choices for the standup location within the narrative flow. They are openers, standup transitions or bridges, and closers.

The general rule is to avoid standup opens. The reason—your face is not the most interesting video.

For the content of standup bridges, look for a way to make a natural transition between points in the story. It could tie together two locations, time frames, or subtopics of the story theme. For instance, in a story with two locations, you'll want to do the standup bridge at the beginning of the sequence of the second location. Then decide if you want camera motion (pans or tilts), lens movement (zoom in or zoom back), or reporter activity (walk and talks, arm motions, pointing). For any movement, there must be a reason to draw the camera's focus from one point to the other.

In some cases, you may want to bridge into a soundbite from an interview that is already on tape. That means the last sentence of the bridge must include the writeup.

If you do that, also shoot a bridge standup without the writeup. You may have to dump the interview and you'll have a safety backup.

For standup closers, the standard is to talk about the future. For that reason, do the standup in a location related to the story, one that might even have some activity in the background.

It is crucial, though, not to think the standups are mandatory parts of breaking news. Don't be afraid to dump outdated standups.

Be Realistic About the Field Video Material

Start by checking out your best video sequence. Is it intriguing enough to open the story? If not, is there some other powerful video that you can move up? If you punt and do this, you'll have to backtrack and redesign the story.

Then go to the sound interviews.

Examine the interviews for powerful answers to how and why questions. Look for telling emotionally strong bites in the :10 to :15 range.

Look for bites that advance the story. Finding a few of these will cut down on the number of your tracks.

Evaluate any standups you might have done. Are they worth using?

Evaluate all the other sequences you have. Do you have enough for two tracks, three tracks, or more? Be realistic. There's nothing more damaging than stretching out a story over a weak series of similar looking shots. The video you have determines how many tracks you can write.

Tracks

The narration written for most short packages forms a checkerboard of tracks interwoven with soundbites or natural sound sequences. Each track covers a stretch from the beginning of the package to the first bite, from soundbite to soundbite, and from the last soundbite to either the story's end or the closing standup. Each track may repeat a few words from the previous soundbite and then include new information and the writeup to the next soundbite.

Most novice reporters encounter two problems when writing tracks. First, they tend to overwrite their tracks, extending beyond what the field video, B-roll or archival visuals will support. They jam too much information into the tracks, stretching out the story and possibly upsetting any sense of pacing. Initial tracks should be :20 or less. Interior tracks are often much shorter, and sometimes are only a phrase as they serve as a **bridge** between two soundbites.

Also, beginning reporters write tracks about story elements for which there is no video. Covering tracks with wallpaper video might dull the audience interest. If you are short on video, put some information in the studio lead-in or tag.

Here are some thoughts about tracks.

Keep Your Tracks Short

Writing short tracks (10 seconds or less) sets up a quicker pace and allows you to rely more on your video's natural sound. It also keeps the sequences short. If you are writing a track and it goes beyond :20, then you should probably revisit it.

Be Wary of Lists in Tracks

If you write a list into a track, you are forcing your editor to find B-roll to match the list. And if this doesn't exist in your field video, then you have written yourself into a corner. Alternatively, you could get an interviewee to say this list, or put it in a standup transition. Here's an example:

Track 2

> BUT THE SCHOOL DISTRICT SAID THERE WERE ONLY THREE OPTIONS:
> BUY A NEW SCHOOL SITE
> GET TEMPORARY CLASSROOMS
> OR SPEND A LOT TO FIX THE OLD SCHOOL.

If you write this list into a track and only have video of the old school, then the audience will be confused by looking at the third item on the list while you are narrating the first two options.

Focus on Solid Writeups to Introduce Bites

Although lower-third CGs will identify the speakers, it often is necessary to introduce the agenda for the bite. Work hard on tight writeup lines that transition to the next bite.

Avoid questions in the writeup. If your writeup is a question, your voice naturally rises at the end. If you don't nail it when recording the tracks, it may sound insincere. So skip the rhetoricals and make the writeups complete and short sentences. Here's an example:

> **Avoid:** AND SO . . . WHAT DID THE FIRE OFFICIALS DO?
> (bite) "The chief and the captains have recommended training all as EMTs. The training will start immediately."

Instead, change this to a simple sentence:

> **Use this instead:** AND SO . . . THE DEPARTMENT OFFICIALS MADE A CHOICE.
> (bite) "The chief and the captains have recommended training all as E-M-Ts. The training will start immediately."

If possible, avoid a writeup that stops abruptly. Sometimes the bite is so convoluted you can only use a part of it. Avoid the temptation to start the sentence in the writeup and let the bite finish it. Often, the track will sound awkward if this constructed continuity doesn't quite mesh up.

>**Avoid:** THE CHIEF AND THE CAPTAINS...
>(bite) "... have recommended training all as E-M-Ts. The training will start immediately."

>**Use:** THE DEPARTMENT WILL GIVE EVERYONE THE E-M-T COURSE.
>(bite) "The training will start immediately."

Write Your First Track With the On-cam Studio Lead-in in Mind

Almost every broadcast field report is preceded by a studio introduction, read by the newscaster, called the lead-in. If the lead-in is carefully written, it can both provide information and carry the audience to the story.

A lead-in has many functions. Fundamentally, it prepares the ground without telling the story. If it gives a short version of the story, why should the listeners or viewers wait for the field report?

Also, it serves as an attention-narrowing funnel, with the wide view in the first sentence and a more specific focus immediately before the package.

The lead-in can be a place to put crucial story information that might not fit in the field report. This often is an update of the story, which works well as the lead-in to a backgrounder.

Finally, the lead-in identifies the next voice that is coming. Usually that is the reporter; however, if the field report opens with a bite before the first track, then the lead-in will be a writeup to the first video soundbite.

Laying Out the Story

This is the simple part. Use the spoken narrative model from chapter 8 that starts with the present and then continues to the scope and then the conflicts or challenges before ending with the future.

- In your mind or on paper, compose a studio anchor lead-in. In the lead-in you want to prepare the audience for your first video, not give it away.

- Next, outline the story on a screen page or a paper page. Start with your intriguing opening sequence and any soundbite you need to augment this. You may need the "why" of the angle here.

- Now, go to the *end* and select elements for the "future" segment.

- Position your strong soundbites to anchor story segments.

- Finally, add the video sequences to coordinate with the story flow. (See Figure 13.1.)

Select first video	Select text for future	Bites & Standup	Write Tracks
Establishing seq.	Establishing seq.	Establishing seq. **Bite 1** **Standup** **Bite 2** Future	Establishing seq. & Track 1 **Bite 1** Track 2 **Standup** Track 3 **Bite 2** Track 4 Future
	Future		

Figure 13.1 Four basic steps to laying out and writing reporter packages.

Next, Write the Tracks

When you are doing tracks, you are writing for the ear, not the page. So, your sentences should follow the rules of dialogue, not prose.

Example of a short package script. This is the beginning of a typical hard news package. It is for the morning package after a fire the previous evening.

Studio Lead-in

FIRE OFFICIALS MAY HAVE THE ANSWER TO WHAT CAUSED NEAR-LY A MILLION DOLLARS DAMAGE TO A DOWNTOWN BUILDING LAST NIGHT.
ROB BOLIN REPORTS.

Track 1

THE OLD WAREHOUSE ON WALLY STREET HAD BEEN VACANT FOR YEARS. SHORTLY AFTER SEVEN P-M . . . IT SUDDENLY WENT UP IN FLAMES.
CAFE OWNER MARIO BIANTIN WATCHED THE BLAZE FROM ACROSS THE STREET.

Bite 1

"One second everything was quiet and the next . . . there were flames coming out the windows and roof . . . even before the fire trucks got here."

Track 2

FIREMEN SAY THE BUILDING WAS FULLY INVOLVED WHEN THEY ARRIVED.
FIRE CAPTAIN ALDEN CARTER SAYS THE WAREHOUSE COULDN'T BE SAVED.

Bite 2

"This type of building has no fire walls and once the thing gets roaring, it's like a locomotive. Nothing can stop it."

Track 3

THE FLAMES COULD BE SEEN FOR MILES AND THE SMOKE BLEW DIRECTLY ACROSS THE BARNES EXPRESSWAY . . . CHOKING OFF TRAFFIC AT THE END OF THE EVENING RUSH HOUR.
IT TOOK THREE HOURS BEFORE THE ROAD WAS OPEN AGAIN.

Standup bridge (flames are out . . . shot in morning)

AS DAWN BROKE . . . ARSON INVESTIGATORS PICKED THROUGH THE BURNED OUT BUILDING. THEY CONCENTRATED THEIR EFFORTS IN ONE CORNER BY THE STREET.

Bite 3

"It looks like it started in this area where transients sleep. We found gasoline and an old camp stove."

Track 4

THE BUILDING'S OWNER SAYS THE FIRE MAY HAVE SAVED HIM SOME TROUBLE. YESTERDAY . . . HE TOOK OUT A PERMIT TO BEGIN THE COSTLY JOB OF TEARING DOWN THE PLACE. THAT WILL HAPPEN NEXT MONTH. THIS IS ROB BOLIN FOR K-560 NEWS.

▶ **EXERCISE 13-B**

Review and Comment on This Package's Tracks

In this exercise, you will act as a producer or editor. You are looking at a first attempt at Track 1 for an environmental story about a homeowner-installed gray water recapture system. The bite is from Lindy Partridge, homeowner, who has re-piped her shower and bathtub to drain that water to a holding tank and eventually to use it for irrigation. The video in the sequence starts CU on the sprinkler watering her lawn for :07, then :10 of a sequence of her holding a hose watering the garden. Can you use the track as written or do you need to change it?

Studio lead-in

SCIENTISTS TODAY RELEASED A STUDY SAYING RAINFALL TOTALS WILL SHRINK IN THE NEXT THREE YEARS.

AND AS HOLDEN PLATFORM REPORTS . . . ONE EAST BAY WOMAN IS DOING HER BEST TO GET READY.

Fade up to :03 of NAT sound of sprinkler.

A LOT OF WATER CAN BE SAVED BY A HOMEOWNER TAKING ADVANTAGE OF CONTRA COSTA COUNTY'S NEW GRAY WATER RECONSTITUION ORDINANCE.

THIS WAS ACCOMPLISHED BY HOMEOWNER LINDY PATRIDGE WITH A MODICUM OF GARAGE IMPLEMENTS . . . SOME ELEMENTARY HAND TOOLS . . . LENGTHS OF PVC-2160 PIPE AND A FIRED UP DETERMINATION TO SAVE WATER.

NOW . . . SHE HAS SUFFICIENT RESOURCES TO PUT IN AN EXPANSIVE GARDEN.

Bite

"Very little. I wouldn't be surprised if we are down to 10 percent of what we used last year. This will really help my grandchildren."

....

....

....

....

....

....

....

....

▶ **EXERCISE 13-C**

Writing a Package Script

Write a :10 lead-in and a 1:20 package for this situation. You have three bites and you will need four tracks. You can use the bites in any order you wish. You may also invent sequences you will need and would like to have. Write the fantasy sequences in parentheses at the beginning of each track.

Situation Notes

You have three soundbites on the story about the supervisors getting ready to vote on a new downtown height limit for buildings in one neighborhood—the Rose District. This is coming up for a vote tonight but everyone thinks it will pass.

   The new plan will allow 24-story buildings in the Rose District, which is an older part of town adjacent to the new high-rise buildings in the Center District. Currently the Rose has a two-story height limit but the new plan will allow 24-story buildings in the area, which is now a hodgepodge of older bungalow style homes. Needless to say, all of the labor unions and construction-related businesses are for the plan. Most of the supervisors appear to like the idea. Neighborhood residents have been fighting the plan, but this is a working class district and they don't have much clout with city hall. They haven't been able to raise enough money to really fight it.

The bites:

Supervisor Rod Stern TRT :08 "We must move ahead with building in this city. No district can tie our hands because they don't want development there."

   Architect Anna Chavez-Rinaldo TRT :13 "It doesn't mean there will be a flood of skyscrapers built there. There are plenty of limits on the bulk of buildings anywhere in town."

   Long-time resident Maria Ramirez TRT :10 "Sure, the supervisors are going to go ahead and hand over our district to the developers. They all live in Mar Vista Estates, which you can bet will stay two stories."

....
....
....
....
....
....
....

Chapter Summary

Shooting, designing, and writing video packages is the reporter's principal assignment. Great care must be taken on location to gather enough sequences and significant bites to eventually construct an engaging package.

Packages are most easily assembled by choosing the opening sequence, setting in the last segment outlining the future, adding golden soundbites that will influence the story design, and then finishing the visual narrative with strong sequences.

Live Shots and Remote Live Reporting

Evolving technology over the past 40 years is making it more certain than ever that live shots or live remotes will be staples in broadcast news. Managers like them because they demonstrate competitive on-the-scene credibility.

These stories are usually completed under intense deadline pressure and often involve complex production with video fed from field sources.

Glossary

DONUT The complete live shot report. Donut refers to a live open and closer from the field.

Q & A Question and Answer. Usually this is planned or scripted.

ROLL CUES The scripted setup phrase that alerts the studio director where to add video and sound.

SANDBAG The surprise question to a live reporter that is not discussed beforehand.

Live Remotes Are Popular

Portable microwave equipment first became popular four decades ago. Stations using it suggested to the audience that the on-the-scene reporting was something they could expect on almost every story.

Now the technology is cheaper, portable uplinks exist, and there are Internet options for routing signals. A two-person crew with a satellite phone setup can report from anywhere in the world. It's called extending the studio.

Local reporters need to have thick skins about live shots. News managers and producers want as many live inserts as possible, even on stories long since over. Often, reporters must do teases and then repeated and varied reports for different newscasts. And they may have to do reports for out-of-town stations with which their station has reciprocal agreements. (See Figure 14.1.)

Figure 14.1 Two-shot screen showing studio anchor tossing to live reporter in the field (courtesy KPIX).

Going Live Creates Intense Pressure

These live cameras come with pitfalls, ethical problems, and production screw-ups. The deadline stress on field crews is crushing. Reporters often arrive on the scene minutes before the first live shot. While the crew is setting up, there is very little time to do any on-the-ground reporting. At times, reporters are forced to repeat information fed to them by producers at the station. The first video transmissions are rough and incomplete. Control room to location production communications are hit and miss.

Production and Ethical Dilemmas

Aside from production, there are many content problems as well. News staffs need to guard that the editorial scrutiny is not compromised. Because so much of the report comes from a live standup in the field, supervision over the story's details is often clumsy. Although there are cellular phones and portable fax machines for scripts, errors can creep into the story.

When faced with a live shot, assignment editors and producers must always ask if there are more effective and economical ways of telling the story. Will there be better clarity and presentation from the studio? Sometimes, they may have to argue against station policies for extensive live coverage.

Producers must be cautious about hype and overuse of the "live" possibility for stories. Although live shots can be wonderfully effective as a means of expanding the studio, care should be taken that the technology is not used merely as a means of advertising the news staff.

Finally, there is the ethical dilemma of being used. Anyone in broadcast journalism is aware that newsmakers in the community begin events to coincide with live newscasts, playing to the known need for live shots during the program. Was the picket line set up at 6 p.m. because that's when the news is on the air? Did the school board schedule a vote at 10:30 to coincide with the 11 o'clock news? Because everyone is aware of this, it is important for reporters and producers to consider to what extent they are being used.

Probably the most ironic live coverage came in 1992 in Somalia, when U.S. Navy SEALS teams landed on a Somali beach and found themselves arriving to television lights, squads of reporters, and CNN live coverage to worldwide television screens. To be accurate, American military press officers had alerted the crews to the landing, but did not expect the turnout that happened.

Live Shot Possibilities

Once the crew establishes a clear signal to the station, the location live shot can take many forms. It can be anything from a field-based mini-newscast to a routine studio toss to live shot, video insert, live tag, and back to the studio. Many times, it moves along so smoothly that the audience isn't aware of the planning and technology needed to produce it. The live shot format has many possibilities.

- A standup with no video

- A standup with the reporter doing a VO

- A standup with the reporter doing a VO/SOUND/VO

- A standup wrapped around a package (called a donut)

- A "Q & A" or "debrief" with the reporter

- Live interview by the reporter

- A reporter split screen with another reporter

- A reporter working as part of a round robin, and tossing to another reporter

- A standup with video fed from the field

- A standup using video pre-fed and edited at the station

The format combinations are fascinating and a little risky. It is crucial that writers and producers simplify when possible and communicate with reporters about what material is available. Are the VO pictures usable? Was everything usable that was fed from the location? Do we have a roll cue? Is the anchor going to ask questions? Will these be questions for which the reporter knows the answers? Or, does the reporter's location presence at night conflict with the information from a day story. (See Figure 14.2).

Writing strategies are as endless as the format combinations. In some ways, live shots give the reporters latitude in story assembly. Live shot formatting is less rigid, and, except for the video work in the donut insert, the structure can be informal. Quite often the field crews and the studio technical staff are winging it.

Figure 14.2 Field reporter on live nightside standup. He included a VO/SOUND segment in this report (courtesy KPIX).

Some Important Rules for Live Shot Design

- The studio toss to the reporter should not steal the reporter's story. The reporter should suggest the toss and the producer must concentrate on getting it right so the story will flow smoothly into the field open. With this in mind, the studio toss must not surprise the reporter.

- The field open should always start with the current situation. Saying something like "IT'S QUIET RIGHT NOW BUT JUST THREE HOURS AGO . . ." helps explain why a reporter is standing at night in an empty field when everyone else has gone home.

- Get to the donut's video as soon as possible. It can be set up as a VO into a tracked package and then switch to a VO at the end, or it can be set up with a natural sound buffer at the top and then be a completely tracked package without a standup.

- The field tag or closer should report the future and the reporter should be ready for a Q & A if that has been set up. However, the anchors should be cautioned against spontaneous questions in areas not discussed beforehand. Sandbagging your reporter will make him or her lose credibility if they cannot answer the question.

Script format varies from station to station; however, most examples have the normal lead-in, notes about the field intro script, and then the all-important cues to the time to roll, insert sound and CGs, and return to live and return to studio.

A sample live shot script might look like this:

O/C   POLICE IN DOWNY FALLS HAVE BROKEN UP
                                   WHAT IS BEING CALLED THE LARGEST DRUG
                                   LAB EVER FOUND IN CLAY COUNTY.

	AUTHORITIES HAVE ARRESTED 12 SUSPECTS AND SEIZED OVER ONE MILLION DOLLARS WORTH OF LAB EQUIPMENT.
	REPORTER MARCUS BROWN IS STANDING BY LIVE.
	MARCUS?
REMOTE ON CAM	(REM)
	POLICE HERE TONIGHT AREN'T SAYING HOW THEY FOUND THE LAB . . . BUT ONLY THAT IT WAS A LONG INVESTIGATION.
VO	(VO)

Pics of police carrying boxes from suburban house

	ALL DAY LONG . . . THE CRIME LAB HAS BEEN LOADING UP EVIDENCE AND TAKING SAMPLES FROM THIS HOUSE IN THE ROSE DISTRICT.
	A POLICE SPOKESMAN SAID IT TOOK THEM A LONG TIME TO BUST THIS OPERATION.
SOT (begins)	SOT
	(police captain Elroy Hirsch) **"We've been after them for two years but we really hit the jackpot here."**

Track 1

Pics of evidence spread out on a table

	AND QUITE A JACKPOT IT WAS. OVER ONE MILLION DOLLARS WORTH OF EQUIPMENT AND FINISHED DRUGS WORTH OVER TWO MILLION DOLLARS ON THE STREET.
	POLICE SAY THE CASE IS PRETTY GOOD AGAINST THE SUSPECTS.
SOUND (continues)	SOUND UP
	(District Attorney Wade Wilson) **"We have twelve suspects and all are being charged with felonies. I think we've got the central core of this operation."**
VO	VO

Pics of suspects walking out of courtroom

	NOW THE ARRAIGNMENT FOR ALL SUS-PECTS IS SET FOR NEXT TUESDAY.
REMOTE ON CAM	(REM ON CAM)
	POLICE STILL AREN'T SAYING IF THERE WILL BE MORE ARRESTS. THAT'S ALL FROM HERE TO-NIGHT . . . THIS IS MARCUS BROWN REPORTING FROM THE ROSE DISTRICT.

▶ **EXERCISE 14-A**

Live Shot Exercise

As a reporter, you need to turn out a live-shot script to cover this situation. You are standing at 10 p.m. in the empty parking lot outside the civic auditorium in the suburbs of your city.

Situation Notes

Noted television producer of violent programs Edina Barnes has now come out against the gunplay and murders on the tube. She is staging a nationwide speaking tour, saying that all of her scripts from now on will feature endings that involve what is called "conflict resolution," a means of defusing tensions. She is speaking tonight at a local civic auditorium and has a wildly enthusiastic audience applauding everything she says. For visuals you have a number of scenes from her earlier violent programs, some file tape of a network executive testifying before a congressional committee about violence, some natural SOT of her speech tonight, and some shots of people watching television at a local electronics sales store.

BARNES SOT :10 "I just hope it isn't too late to reverse the damage that I have done."

NETWORK EXEC Adrianne Lister "Miss Barnes's conversion comes at an odd time, just when her string of endless trashy programs was losing audience appeal. We are waiting to see how genuine it is."

PSYCHOLOGIST Helen Goertz "It's been clear for a long time that children are deeply affected by violence on television."

....

....

....

▶ **EXERCISE 14A** *continued*

....

....

....

....

....

....

....

....

....

....

Chapter Summary

The live shot or live remote is a common format used in broadcast and online news. With the proper equipment, this type of location reporting becomes an extension of the studio.

The live shot complexity can range from a simple standup to a mini-newscast with VO and tracked packages inserted from a control room. Reporters and producers must be aware that media savvy event planners take news broadcast times into consideration.

15

Producers Develop Individual Stories

The previous chapters focused on the newswriter or reporter, but this chapter is aimed at the producer.

The producer is the gatekeeper, the editor, the story developer, the resources coordinator, the copyeditor, the legal backstop, and the person responsible for the newscast quality and production. The producer may assign stories to writers, select the angle and story length, and then coach the writer through difficult stages of the story before examining the script for accuracy, fairness, comprehensive coverage, perspective, opinion, libel, invasion of privacy, and adherence to station writing style. The finished story is then ready for inclusion in the newscast. Chapter 16 will examine how the newscasts should be structured.

Glossary

ADVANCING THE STORY Updating a story by contacting news sources or providing fresh material.

DAYBOOK An assignment desk file that contains information about stories scheduled for a particular date.

GATEKEEPING The process of selecting, developing, editing, and eventually sequencing stories for the newscast. Gatekeeping also involves eliminating stories.

HFRs Hold for Release. Completed feature or backgrounder stories that can be used with a current breaking news item. Also called evergreens or banked stories.

The Producer as Gatekeeper

The gatekeeper role allows the producer to decide which stories will go into the newscast and then to see that these stories are developed by deadline. To do this, a producer should be current on local, national, and international stories and make decisions about covering scheduled events or breaking stories.

Additionally, a producer should be willing to take chances and go beyond the routine formats to cement a solid journalistic story. A producer should promote enterprise by his or her reporters and staff members, constantly urging them to find new sources, get new reaction, and always advance the story.

The Producer's Many Jobs

Long before a script is copyedited, the producer's stamp goes on each individual story. This begins during the assignment stage, where the producer's needs often require the news department to commit resources needed to obtain expanded story or video coverage.

There are five principal tasks: (1) finding and evaluating stories, (2) developing and assigning stories, (3) coaching and copyediting, (4) stacking the newscast, and (5) making on-air decisions. We will cover 4 and 5 in chapter 16.

The News of the Day

Producers should listen to, watch, and read all major news sources as the day develops, even before they get to the office. Sometimes it is necessary to call the newsroom to see that the major stories are being covered, expanded, and updated. The producer can also check the daybook to see if any events worth covering are scheduled.

At the office, most good producers maintain a list of must run stories and minor stories that will be possibilities for the newscast. One way to do it is to use a simple crosshatch to segregate major and minor stories. (See Figure 15.1.)

The producer carries the story list or rough sheet everywhere, adding to it throughout the day and crossing off stories that don't pan out. Stories in the must run video side or even the must run readers should be constantly developed by looking for outside help in visuals, tape trades, satellite services and network feeds, stringer footage, wire stories, and so on.

Step One Add and prepare the HFR (hold for release) stories you have ready. Make sure the lead-ins are written into script form, the CGs are ordered, and timing is checked on the scripts. These stories can be blocked into your newscast.

Step Two Once you have a lead story in mind, go all out on the coverage of this one. Make certain that there aren't any holes in the journalistic and mechanical coverage of it. Perhaps you need to assign a writer early in the day to tie together all the loose ends of the story.

Must run video	Must run readers
Minor stories with video	Minor reader stories

Figure 15.1 Diagram of a typical producer's rough sheet of story lists.

Step Three Maintain the running list of the minor stories and check this throughout the day to see if you've missed anything. Begin to pass out writing assignments on the more important stories.

Step Four Don't kill any stories until you get near the time for stacking the newscast. It's always better to work with options; however, don't commit writers to marginal stories until you know you'll need those stories.

Finally Don't vacillate. Make decisions and then follow up on them. Say yes or no. Take control of the newscast.

Developing Stories

Producers can develop stories by advancing the information and looking for extra visuals or sidebar stories, interviews, and reports to fill in the gaps. By updating all of the information and double-checking sources, coverage can be expanded. Here are some steps to develop a simple :25 wire story on a forest fire:

1. Contact someone to get visuals of fire. This will provide more information to viewers.

2. Get computer artists to make a map of the area.

3. Have the assignment desk send a reporter to scene. Set up a live report. It will work with a VO and map.

4. Have a writer check out past fires in the area. Pull file video if necessary.

5. Have a reporter set up and feed video for a live shot.

6. Check to see whether any HFRs on fire danger are available. By the end of Step 6, you'll have a studio lead-in with a map, a live shot with a VO/SOT insert, and a backgrounder to follow all that. You'll have easily 6:00 of material. You might have to cut it down.

7. See if the graphic artists can come up with an OTS (over-the-shoulder) topic box for the story. See if there is already one that is usable.

Checking Feeds

Most news stations or agencies have contracts with services that feed national and international stories. These come in package, VO-SOUND, or VO formats. A producer should examine the daily feed's printed rundown for story resources that can either be combined with a local angle or can stand alone as features that are revealing to a local audience. These might involve statewide or national legislation, nationwide school problems, tech stories, health, science, business, or the arts.

Assigning Stories

Once it is certain a story will be in the newscast, the producer can assign a projected total story time, choose a format (READER/VO/VO/SOUND/LIVE SHOT), and decide what visuals such as OTS topic boxes and full-screen visuals should be included.

At that point, the producer must assign the writing responsibility to other producers, newswriters, or anchors. At smaller stations, the producer will probably write many scripts.

▶ EXERCISE 15-A

Composing a Story Pool

This exercise can be done by groups or individuals. You are to make up a story pool totaling 10 stories. This may include international, national, regional and local stories. Assume you have access to AP or other newswire services, check the resources available on each topic, and describe how you would advance and expand the story.

....

....

....

....

....

....

....

....

....

....

....

....

Fairness

It is easy to understand how reporters may be sympathetic to a particular argument or political side in a story. However, most news organizations outside of certain 24-hour cable news operations aggressively demand a policy of balanced fairness. Scripts must be checked to see whether writers have made an effort to obtain all sides of a story and have written it without bias.

► **EXERCISE 15-B**

Checking Fairness in Script Copy

Examine this story for fairness. Circle any areas that might need a second look.

O/C A CITIZEN'S ENVIRONMENTAL COMMITTEE IS ACCUSING A RICH-MOND AREA REFINERY OF INTENTIONALLY AND KNOWINGLY LEAK-ING THOUSANDS OF GALLONS OF CHEMICAL WASTE INTO PALAMI-NO CREEK.

  THE GROUP . . . CALLING ITSELF CITIZENS AGAINST POLLUTION . . . OR CAP . . . CHARGES THE FUELEX REFINERY MADE TEN SECRE-TIVE DUMPS OF CHEMICALS IN THE PAST 15-MONTHS.

  A CAP SPOKESWOMAN SAID THE REFINERY RELEASED THE SPILLS AT NIGHT AND FAILED TO NOTIFY THE POLLUTION CONTROL DIS-TRICT.

  THE REFINERY HAD NO RESPONSE.

Chapter Summary

The producer's job begins with a survey of all possible stories for the newscast. From this pool, stories need development to expand their coverage. After writers prepare scripts, the producer needs to check for accuracy, fairness, scope of coverage, and writing style. Producers should also backstop the stories for legal accountability, which is covered in chapter 18.

16

Producing Effective Newscasts

The producer's job is to construct a comprehensive news presentation, whether it is for broadcast or the Internet. Producers must understand limits and qualities of both stories and writers. Certain concerns go into the story order or "stacking" as it is called. Stacking the newscast must be done with an eye to pacing, story rhythm and on-time production.

Glossary

BACKTIME The start time for a newscast story, if the newscast is to end at the scheduled clock time. This process is handled by the computer news systems; however, in smaller stations it might still be done by hand.

CLUSTERING Placing stories with similar themes or topics together in the newscast.

NEWS HOLE The time devoted to news stories in a newscast.

STACKING THE NEWSCAST The procedure for ordering stories within the timed segments of the newscast. Also known as formatting. Normally, the producer or editor stacks the newscast, but at smaller stations, the newscaster may do this.

TEASE A short item that is designed to attract listeners or viewers to a late story in the newscast. In television, video may be used with the tease.

TOSS A short item that is the transition from one newscaster to the other.

General Considerations for Newscast Producers

Noncommercial Versus Commercial News

Producers who work at noncommercial news stations generally have a single running newscast without any breaks. This simplifies the stacking of stories, but also gives the producer little leeway to correct production misfortunes that routinely happen during a live newscast. Noncommercial stations build in routine music pauses and hold features on standby to serve as an emergency filler if a feed machine breaks down or a live remote transmission goes awry.

Producers who work at commercial stations will approach the stacking in a different way. They no longer have a single news flow but a patchwork of segments, sometimes as many as 10 in an hour. Each ad break produces a new segment, and each segment will have its own rationale for story flow. For these, you might have two or three separate lead stories. Generally the segments are designated by letters and the individual stories by numbers. Thus, a story may carry the number B-1 or C-12.

Significant Stories First

Newspapers put the most important stories on the front page. This placement is a cue to the readers about each item's impact. Research has shown that the audience gives more emphasis to stories on the front page.

For broadcast, the position within the newscast also is revealing. Major breaking stories belong at the top of the newscast. The listeners and viewers assume that if you think it's important, you'll put it first. It can be any topic, but it must have weight. Lighter human interest stories, science, and the arts are relegated to the closing segments.

Backgrounders in the Middle

Producers fill the middle of the newscast with longer and more complex stories that explain conditions or change within the community. Usually these lack hard immediacy but are major investigations, profiles, obits, enterprise features, science updates, education, or stories about community issues.

Upbeat and Feature Stories Later

The last third of a newscast is generally a good spot to run cultural stories, advancers for community events, and lighter human interest features. Because it is a portion that winds down emotionally, it is understandable that tragedy should be avoided here.

Warm, upbeat features called kickers usually finish off the last segment. Critics have charged that news producers go looking for these light stories and exclude more important news to continue a preordained newscast formula. As long as a producer remains flexible, using features and kickers at the conclusion is not a bad use a newscast's time constraints. Anyone who offers the public repetitive sameness of a single category of news is also guilty of finding stories to fit a mold. On heavy news days, you can vary the proportion of major stories to features. On light news days, the proportion floats the other way.

Clustering

It makes sense that stories of a similar nature or theme should be clustered to help the audience focus on the issues.

This can be controversial. Minor stories attached to major stories often are given too much importance, even if the theme or topic is similar. Five crime stories in a row, four fire stories, or three back-to-back recreation stories will not serve your purposes.

An acceptable compromise might be to look for short clusters, but stack them cautiously, including them in the newscast only when the stories are of equal weight and topic. Limit the clusters to two stories.

Headlining Stories That Come Later

Often, long-running stories like the BP gulf oil spill get overexposure over a period of weeks. Acknowledging that these stories are important, but not wanting to dedicate the entire first half of the newscast to this one story day after day, producers can headline the BP oil spill story at the top and tease to an expanded story later. This is a good compromise that continues the story coverage while allowing the audience to hear a variety of other news.

Wraps

In producing, wraps are two or three similar topic stories that you will combine into one all-inclusive story. This differs from a cluster that runs individually formatted stories in adjacent slots. Wraps merge two or three stories under a common lead into a single tightly formatted story.

For instance, a wrap may bring together three minor fire stories, all with VOs, resulting in a newsreel look. The new story would get a slug of Wrap/Fire, have a TST of :40, and include three separate items. Wraps are handy formats, but can seem overdone if too many appear in one newscast.

Segues

Producers need to be on the lookout for possible segues. These transitions will use clusters to interweave a stacking order based on geography or theme. Go from an international story on exports to a local business story with an export angle. Follow a statewide story on school funding with one on local school decisions. The stories are not exactly clustered but are still tied, and segues can give you a smooth transition between anchors.

Single Versus Multiple Anchors

A single anchor newscast is easy to organize. All graphics have the same screen vector and face a certain way. There are no tosses, and the single anchor's reading speed is easily figured into the timing. Other than pacing the stories, little design goes into completing the rundown or stack of the newscast.

A double or multiple anchor newscast provides the producer with a myriad of questions. How often do we make the change from one anchor to the other? Will it be a toss or spilt story to make the shift? Will we shift coming out of a story, or package, or should both anchors be on camera at any particular time? If so, are the cameras available and not being used for side anchors? Most of these decisions are built into the format, but each requires an extra amount of plotting and design.

Pacing

Producers, anchors, and news directors forever argue about the pacing—the rhythm and flow of the newscast. On strong news days when you have multiple consensus lead stories, all with active videotape, live shots, Q & A interviews, and sidebars, the producer can storm ahead without fear.

But on slow news days, when even the lead story is debatable, the producer has to work to keep up the pace. This involves a strategy that alternates readers, VOs, VO/SOUND, live shots, and packages while carefully placing short topic clusters. It is always subject to post-newscast second-guessing. Producers die a thousand deaths on the anemic news days.

Predictability

There are different theories about how predictable a newscast should be. Some producers set up segments exactly the same way every day. First segment, 8:00, opens with anchor A reading a breaking local story (doesn't have to be a major one), switches to B for one national story, switches back to A for local story with videotape package, switches to B for two local VOs, switches back to A for another local package (upbeat), and then B does the tease across break and before commercial. Second segment starts on A with wrap of three national stories, then to B, and so on.

Although it's nice to have a fallback format, it's a shame to get locked into it. Producers should make an extra effort to avoid simply plugging stories into a preordained format.

Avoid predictable ping-ponging. On newscasts with a double anchor format, producers often switch anchors on almost every story to keep up the pacing. Known as ping-ponging, too much of it becomes very disconcerting. A solution is to vary the number of stories each anchor reads, avoid predictable changes, and when the anchor reads a second or even a third story in a row, to turn the anchor to another camera.

Teases

Part of a producer's job is to write the teases. These are formatted story positions before the newscast or before commercial breaks within the newscast. The well-written tease is a valuable tool for smoothing the continuity. Research has shown it is beneficial to present an audience with an agenda and teases accomplish this.

The essence of good tease writing is to offer highlights of the story without giving away the details or the results of any actions. A tease with too many details would sound like this:

THE AIRCRAFT CARRIER SEAGULL IS HOME AGAIN AFTER A SIX-MONTH TOUR IN THE MIDDLE EAST. THAT STORY IS COMING UP.

A better tease would refer to the story and tap into keywords that might interest many. Try this one:

A JOYFUL HOMECOMING FOR MANY NAVY FAMILIES. THAT STORY IS COMING UP.

Great care must be used to avoid slamming your audience with a sensationalized tease. Viewers and listeners can be offended if the tease doesn't live up to its hype.

ALL OF DOWNTOWN IS DESTROYED BY FIRE. THAT STORY IS COMING UP NEXT.

Viewers wait for the story only to find that it is a downtown in a remote Peruvian village. They feel cheated and rightly so.

Producers must be cautious they don't reveal a story result in the tease. Better to leave it up in the air. For instance

THE ZONING BOARD VOTES TO APPROVE THE NEW MALL NIGHT-CLUB. THAT STORY IS NEXT.

In this tease, you've told them the story. They don't have to stick around for the news story that's coming next. You can avoid this by leaving it uncertain.

THE ZONING BOARD MAKES A CONTROVERSIAL DECISION ON THE MALL NIGHTCLUB. THAT STORY IS NEXT.

▶ **EXERCISE 16A**

Writing Teases

Study the situations. Prepare a short tease for each situation to alert viewers that the story is coming up later in the newscast.

Situation Notes 1

A local citizens' crime study committee has suggested a review of the management policies of the chief of police

....
....
....
....

Situation Notes 2

Thieves vandalized a local church just two days before a big holiday that celebrated the Church community's ethnic history.

....

....

....

....

Situation Notes 3

A well-known and local semiprofessional baseball team needs one more league win to make it to the league finals in the state capital.

....

....

....

....

Situation Notes 4

Former members of a cult with local ties to your city are taking their guru to court, claiming he imprisoned them and wouldn't let them leave the group's mountain retreat.

....

....

....

....

Situation Notes 5

Air Force One, with the president on board, comes within a half mile of colliding with a small private plane near the Denver Airport.

....

....

....

....

Tosses

A toss between newscasters on the set or with a reporter in the field should be informal and carefully scripted. The producer should make certain that the toss doesn't give away the story or surprise the reporter. Here are some format variations:

- *Ad lib toss.* Writing the words "ad lib toss" on a script page is a recipe for disaster. It is risky because newscasters often are busy and don't have the time to come up with a clever ad lib toss. If you assign an ad lib toss, be prepared for catastrophe.

- *Toss to personality.* This often signals that the producer has run out of ideas for a toss. "NOW HERE'S REPORTER LUCY WATKINS WITH A STORY ON CATTLE." Not very exciting.

- *Toss to the story.* This is one of the two viable methods of connecting one anchor to a reporter. It's a good idea to always toss to the story and then include the reporter's name.

  > IT'S NOT OFTEN WE SEE ELEPHANTS ON THE STREETS OF RIVER-
  > DALE. REPORTER LARRY DOVBRUSH HAS THAT STORY.
  > LARRY?

- *The split-story toss.* Both anchors appear in a two-shot. The first anchor reads the headline or top half of the story. The second anchor picks up the story and turns to a camera and completes it on a single anchor shot. This is an easy and very effective shift.

Anchor A	RESIDENTS IN RIVERDALE MIGHT HAVE BLINKED TWICE WHEN THEY SAW A HERD OF ELEPHANTS TRAMPLING LAWNS IN THEIR NEIGHBORHOOD THIS MORNING.
Anchor B	YES . . . BUT THEY WERE OUT THERE FOR A GOOD REASON AND REPORTER LARRY DOVBRUSH IS STANDING BY WITH THAT STORY. LARRY?

► **EXERCISE 16-B**

Writing Tosses

Write a split-story toss for two anchors with these situation notes.

Situation Notes

This is a story about tearing down a historic city library branch to build a new high-tech building. The city planning commission has voted 5-4 to allow the city to demolish the structure. Neighborhood preservationists who fought this for at least a year now say they will appeal this ruling to a state court. The city attorney, interviewed by anchor B, says they have no legal standing to fight the decision and that the planning commission's vote is the final word.

....

....

....

....

....

....

....

....

Junk Pages

Teases, tosses, hellos, opens, and goodbyes occupy a page slot and are routine production scripts that are often called the junk pages. They retain the same basic makeup day after day. Producers simply fill in the blanks with a new reference for each newscast.

Stacking the Newscast

Stacking means sequencing the stories in the newscast rundown. A producer must consider anchor assignments, story content, topic clusters, story length, and a pleasant rhythm of visual stories. The stories are placed among commercial spots, teases, special segments such as sports or weather, and tosses.

Figuring the News Hole

The first step in producing is to find out how much news you will need for the newscast that day. Finding the actual length of the news hole is a simple process.

Take the station log for the newscast and subtract the time the newscast goes on the air from the time it goes off and you will have the length of the newscast. From that number, subtract any commercials; the junk pages of teases, hellos, and goodbyes; theme music; credits; and regularly produced features such as sports and weather. What is left is called the news hole. This is the amount of time you need to find news stories to fill.

Here's an example for a half-hour newscast:

Goes on the air at	11:00:40
Goes off the air at	11:28:40
—————Subtract—————	
Newscast is	28:00
Subtract junk pages (1:00)	27:00
Subtract sports, wx (4:00)	23:00
Subtract ads (10:00)	13:00
News hole is	13:00

That means you have only 13 minutes of news in your half-hour newscast. Producers must apportion this time out among the selected stories.

Update the Story Pool

A good place to start is to list the possible stories on a producer's rough sheet (see chapter 15). Here's a list of some stories to be used in the next exercise. Call it the workbook story pool. These stories are listed in random order.

The pool of news stories for our stacking exercise:

- *Mayor's trip/package.* Mayor Bowman has returned from ten-city trip to promote your city's industry. She claims to have opened new markets.

- *Out-of-town ax/VO.* A 35-car accident on a nearby metro area freeway left two dead and tied up the major interchange for 12 hours.

- *Crime spree/reader.* Two escapees from a state prison have terrorized the northern part of your state, the most recent a bank robbery yesterday.

- *Economic predictions/reader.* A local bank says the regional economy will grow through the next fiscal year. The job market will be better.

- *Transit mess/reader.* Consultants say the local Rapid Transit Bus System is poorly managed and is burdened with sky-high unfunded pension and health benefits.

- *City budget/package.* Next year's budget will hold the line on taxes but will cut 10 percent of the police force and school budget to save money.

Must run video		Must run readers
MAYOR	PKG	Transit
CITY BUDGET	PKG	Crime Spree
AMBULANCE	VO	Recall
		Reading

Minor stories with video		Minor reader stories
TICKERS	VO	Fraud
CAR INTO BANK	PKG	Economy
METRO AX	VO	State Budget

Figure 16.1 A first outline of the story pool on a typical rough sheet.

- *Fraud trial/reader.* A former city attorney's trial continues. He is charged with taking an aged client's money from her trust account.

- *Ambulance service/VO.* City officials investigate charges that the ambulance service response time is high and that the vehicles are underequipped.

- *Car into bank/package.* A motorist's foot slipped from the brake and the car crashed into the lobby of a local bank. No one hurt. Damage minor.

- *State budget/reader.* It's up 21 percent this year, mostly for higher salaries. The state hopes to get the new money by raising property taxes.

- *Reading scores/reader.* Reading scores are up for all grades at local schools. Superintendent Lyle Whippem credits a back-to-basics approach.

- *Tickets/VO.* City traffic officials announced they are raising the cost of a parking ticket to $35 from $25. This, they hope, will raise additional $$.

From the story pool, divide the stories into categories on the producer's rough sheet. Identify which are must run stories and which are the less important. Here's an example of the list on a rough sheet breakdown. (See Figure 16.1.)

Find the Leads

Next, select stories that are possible lead caliber. From our story pool this might be the mayor's trip, the city budget, or the crime spree.

Assign Times and Check Totals

The news hole is 13:00. Now you want to start assigning story lengths and possible formats. If you don't reach the total of 13:00, start to plug in minor stories. (See Figure 16.2.)

At this point, you have 13:40 of stories to fill 13:00. We've ordered a package on the READING story and there is a possibility that you will pick up additional stories or expand current ones by adding more elements. This means you will need to cut out items or reduce story times already allocated.

Figure 16.2 The stories have now been given a format and ballpark TST.

1.	CITY BUDGET	PKG	2:30
2.	Crime Spree	Read	0:45
3.	MAYOR TRIP	PKG	2:45
4.	State Budget	Read	0:30
5.	Recall	Read	0:30
6.	AMBULANCE	VO	0:45
7.	METRO AX	VO	0:45
8.	CAR INTO BANK	PKG	1:30
9.	Transit	Read	0:30
10.	READING	PKG	2:00
11.	Economy	Read	0:30
12.	TICKETS	VO	0:40

Figure 16.3 The actual stacking of the stories with anchor assignments on the left.

A	1.	MAYOR TRIP	PKG	2:30
B	2.	Crime Spree	Read	0:45
A	3.	CITY BUDGET	PKG	2:30
A	4.	State Budget	Read	0:30
B	5.	Recall	Read	0:30
B	6.	AMBULANCE	VO	0:30
A	7.	METRO AX	VO	0:45
A	8.	CAR INTO BANK	PKG	1:30
B	9.	Transit	Read	0:30
B	10.	TICKETS	VO	0:30
A	11.	Economy	Read	0:30
B	12.	READING	PKG	2:00

Re-stack and Adjust the Story Times to Complete the Rundown

Now you re-order stories and adjust times and sketch out a rundown. For this newscast, we've shortened the Mayors Trip, the Ambulance and the Tickets story. Give these new times to the writers as story lengths. (See Figure 16.3.)

You're on the way. This is a format that fits within the time limits and has a solid story order. It has a producer's selection of important stories in the lead, backgrounders near the middle and a thoughtful story as the segment conclusion. It also has clustering with the city budget series, the mayor's trip series, the ambulance, accident, and car/bank series. It has potential for segues, and it has pacing, with no large blocks of read-only stories.

Reviewing the Scripts

Once the writer submits a script, copyediting must be thorough. The producer or news editor should examine the story for errors of fact, law, and style. If any of these errors in the story are found, the story should be returned to the writer.

Accuracy is the first and the most important consideration in the editing of any story. There can be no compromise in this area. Producers can check for accuracy by

- Reviewing sources. Any doubts about the quality of primary or secondary sources must be conveyed to the audience. Double check source copy.

- Questioning jargon. Is any backgrounding needed?

- Reviewing adjectives or story assumptions.

Producers, if they are separate from copyeditors, must also check all actualities (radio) or visuals (television).

- Checking all video packages. Producers should review the track scripts and look at the package when possible. There should be no surprises in the newscast. Studio lead-ins should be checked for repetition and revealing the story content.

- Every actuality or soundbite must be carefully referenced. Those with no writeup and cold intros must be reviewed.

- Checking visuals. All OTS (over the shoulder) topic boxes must be checked for intent and any full screen CGs must be checked to see if the graphic artist carried out the intent of the newswriter.

▶ **EXERCISE 16-C**

Checking Accuracy Against Source Copy

Review the wire copy to see if the broadcast script that follows is accurate. In this case, the producer assigned a :30 reader.

PARIS, France (RPG)—The health benefits of red wine are in the news again and this time the news is good, according to the French.

At this year's Vinexpo, the world's largest wine exposition held here every two years, scientists and doctors did their best to leave the impression that moderate wine consumption of red wine is great for the health.

The reason for the optimism is a new series of studies that shows that the tannins in red wine increase the amount of free oxygen in the blood and prevent cholesterol pockets from forming, producing an effect similar to aspirin, said Rene Parquet, chief officer of the French wine exporting group Vin Monde.

French officials pointed out that this comes only from red wine and not white, not an unusual claim to be made in this city of Bordeaux, know the world over for its rich red wines.

European grape growers are concerned about new anti-alcohol laws that are popping up in Europe and around the globe. "There has been an increase in alcohol related legislation and it's not been the best for us," said Jacques Jerboa, a leading exporter. "Governments think they can solve their addiction problems by legislating against wine when drugs and cheap alcohol drinks are the problems," he added.

▶ **EXERCISE 16-C** *continued*

Examples of the laws are prohibitions on advertising and sales of alcohol drinks on television and in certain periodicals in countries such as the United States. "These must be carefully reviewed," said one French official.

U.S. importer Vins de France of New Jersey president Robert Vintage said it's unlikely that the new French research will change any laws. "We must learn to get the word out in any way we can, and we'll continue to do this. It's clear the public is happy keeping alcohol advertising off TV, thinking this will stop their kids from drinking," Vintage added.

On Camera   NEW RESEARCH IS SAYING IT'S OKAY TO HAVE A GLASS OF WINE WITH MEALS . . . AND THAT THIS IS REALLY A HEALTH BENEFIT.

THE STUDIES COME FROM FRANCE . . . AND CAME TO LIGHT DURING THE WORLD'S LARGEST INTERNATIONAL WINE EXPOSITION IN BORDEAUX.

RESEARCHERS SAY A SINGLE GLASS OF WINE WILL HELP RELEASE OXYGEN IN THE BLOOD . . . . THAT OXYGEN IS A BIG HELP IN REMOVING SOME OF THE CHOLESTEROL THAT HAS BUILT UP IN ARTERIES.

THE FRENCH SAY IT'S HARD TO GET THE WORD OUT THOUGH.

FRENCH WINE EXECUTIVE ROBERT VINTAGE SAYS THERE ARE TOO MANY LAWS AGAINST WINE ADVERTISING AND THAT SOMETHING SHOULD BE DONE ABOUT IT.

Plausibility

As a journalist, you should have a good idea of the authenticity of the claims made or news in the story.

Your story is only as good as your sources. It is always wise to ask, Do I have the strongest sources for this information? Are you using reliable primary sources, qualified experts, or actual eyewitnesses? Or are you getting the information from someone who heard it from someone who heard it from someone?

▶ **EXERCISE 16-D**

Accuracy and Plausibility

Review this story and copyedit it. Review this copy for accuracy, fairness, plausibility, the scope of the story, number style, and all other areas of this chapter.

DRUG/jnh/1pm

SCIENTISTS AT BUREK LABS IN NEW YORK ARE SAYING A NEW ANTI-RASH DRUG IS GIVING EXCITING RESULTS.

SUFFERERS FROM CRIPPLING BOUTS OF POISON OAK AND POISON IVY SHOULD REJOICE. THEIR SUFFERING MAY END SOON.

IN THREE TESTS OVER SIX WEEKS . . . POISON OAK RASHES ON 4,237 RATS WERE AFFECTED 40% OF THE TIME FOR THE ALPHA TEST SEQUENCE AND 21% OF THE TIME FOR THE BETA TEST SEQUENCE. THIS LED RESEARCHERS TO A 3 OUT OF TEN PROBABILITY THAT THE NEW OINTMENT IS EFFECTIVE . . . AT LEAST ON RATS.

HUMAN CLINICAL TESTING BEGINS SOON.

....
....
....
....
....
....
....
....
....

Simplified Newscast Rundown Sheet

Anchor	Page	Slug	TST	Backtime
Lou	A-1	MAYOR	2:30	
Pat	A-2	Crime	0:30	
Lou	A-3	CITY BUDGET	2:30	
Lou	A-4	State Budget	0:45	
Pat	A-5	Recall	0:30	
Pat	A-6	AMBULANCE	0:30	
Lou	A-7	METRO AX	0:45	
Lou	A-8	CARBANK	1:30	23:30
Pat	A-9	Transit	0:30	25:00
Pat	A-10	TICKETS	0:30	25:30
Lou	A-11	Economy	0:30	26:00
Pat	A-12	READING	2:00	26:30
		Off air clock time		28:30

Figure 16.4 An example of how manual backtiming works. The crucial figure is the off-time in relation to real clock time. From this clock time of 28:30, you subtract the TST of the last story READING to get the backtime of 26:30. Then, you continue working your way up the format. The newscast log-on time is 15:30.

Backtiming

Although computers have taken over this chore, the producer should learn to backtime a newscast. The backtime is the clock time a story should begin if the newscast is to end on time (according to the clock—not the newscast duration). It is always computed in real clock time and is always calculated from the end of the newscast, working backward. The backtimes are important if stories must be added or dropped while the newscast is on the air.

You will need the exact TST (total story time) on each story. Putting the story order down on a format sheet prepares you for backtiming. If you are doing this by hand, blank format sheets should always be filled in with a pencil, to allow for scribbling when you change story TSTs and backtimes.

A computer news system takes care of this function automatically. In Figure 16.4, you can see how the subtraction scheme works. Go to the station log time for the end of the newscast 11:28:30 and subtract the TST of the story READING—and you have the backtime or ideal start time for the READING item. To find the backtime for each story, you simply continue up the format, subtracting the story time from the backtime of the story below it. (You might try finishing up the backtimes for the story stack in Figure 16.4.) When you've got the backtime for story A-1, it should match the station log-on time (15:30) for the newscast.

Making Decisions During a Live Newscast

The producer is responsible for the length of the newscast, and often must pull, insert, and alter stories while the program is on the air. Only the producer should make editorial changes in the control room booth during the newscast. Although the studio production director must make some immediate decisions if technical needs change, the director must defer to the producer in questions that concern the newscast's content.

Post-Mortems

Unless it is the 11 p.m. newscast, the producer or executive producer should hold a staff meeting and post-mortem immediately. Writers and anchors should attend if possible. The staff should discuss poorly done stories and look for solutions to production misfires.

▶ **EXERCISE 16-E**

Group Exercise in Stacking a Newscast

Break up into groups of 4. Each group designates a producer, an anchor, and two writers. On a given day and with the instructor's assistance, the group selects a total story pool of 12 separate stories. These should include a few breaking stories, some backgrounders, some local neighborhood items, and a few back-of-the-book arts and culture or human interest features.

Each group will then select four stories to be packages, two to be VOs, and six to be readers. Each group will then apportion out the times to complete a 10:00 news segment and stack the stories in order, keeping in mind that a comfortable rhythm and pacing and a varied selection of story formats should be maintained. When the format is finished, the producers and writers will script the readers, the VOs, and the lead-ins for the packages. The scripts will then be placed in the story list and the anchor will read these in order.

Chapter Summary

The producer must check all stories for accuracy, fairness, scope, libel, and writing style. The producer is responsible for planning stories, developing stories, coaching the writers, assigning times for individual stories, composing the story order for the newscasts, checking to see that all stories are completed, and seeing that the newscast is produced on the air as planned.

17

On-Air News and Website Coordination

The Internet has allowed broadcast news agencies to expand their coverage options and receive good feedback. Many stations have taken advantage of the space on the web to broadcast events live, store raw actualities, and to archive all parts of their newscasts.

This chapter is about the various tactics that make effective use of their Internet home pages.

Glossary

ABOVE THE FOLD A term describing the top portion of a print newspaper front page and the initial home page of an Internet news site.

AIRCHECK An archival recording of an on-air news broadcast.

NAVIGATION The term for moving quickly around a Web site page.

RSS FEEDS An automatic method of syndicating news material that allows other reader sites to assemble it for a user.

Internet Offers Expanded Delivery Channels

For the majority of the 20th century, broadcast news operations sought ways to open up time for more coverage. Stations purchased competing channels, built 24-hour cable operations, usurped lightly watched time periods, expanded evening broadcasts to a maximum length, purchased budget-busting live trucks, and increased the number of personalities on the air.

Then the Internet came of age with its unlimited space, easy interconnections to other sites, and social media. Traditional broadcast stations had three choices—ignore it, compete with it, or embrace it. Those who welcomed it found innovative ways to distribute alternative or community news, weather, traffic, and sports and at the same time provide instant access to live feeds, raw actualities, archival video, and expanded resources for individual stories. Their first experimental efforts have now blossomed into what might be called News 2.0.

The recent saga around the thirty-three trapped Chilean miners and their rescues showed just how far these savvy stations had come. This gripping story needed daily updating over many months and ended with highly technical work deep underground. The story bubbled with sidebar possibilities, backgrounders, personal successes or failures, and technical explanations. On the day of the final rescue, millions around the world watched intermittent broadcast news as well as live Internet feeds as each miner stepped from the life-saving capsule. At the same time, Web sites offered explanations of the technology used, the backstory on the rescue operations, or commentary on the political stake the government had in the operation.

The Convergence of Delivery Options

To use a cliché, the audience is now empowered. They can watch or listen to your on-air news and expand their knowledge by clicking on complementary stories tailored to their needs on your Web site. For broadcast-centric news agencies, the internet adds delivery options while the social media Facebook and Twitter feeds the para-social relationships. This has led to several industry-wide uses.

Stories From the Newscast Shuttled to a Podcast or the Web Site

This is a simple route to take. The story, along with the anchor lead-in video and tag, are excerpted from the newscast aircheck and featured on the Web site or offered as a podcast. This allows time shifting and convenience for those who couldn't see the broadcast. If the lead-in to the story was dated, it can be removed if the first track is comprehensive. If Track 1 is too dependent on a studio intro, then it should be re-tracked to include the information.

Features Originated for the Internet

As we mentioned in chapter 13, feature stories might be left off the newscast, broken apart to run as VO/SOUND pieces, or might be designed for the Internet alone and never considered for air.

In these cases, the engaging ideas that might have made up an anchor's studio lead-in must be interwoven into the first tracks. (See Figure 17.1.)

In the following broadcast story, a studio lead-in kicked off the story:

On Cam   TAMPA RESIDENT CARLY HEINZ LEFT HER APARTMENT
                FRIDAY AND HEADED FOR HER PARKED FORD MUSTANG.
                BUT IT WASN'T IN THE CARPORT AND . . . THE CARPORT
                WASN'T THERE.
                REPORTER FRED LOAM HAS THE STORY OF THE AMAZ-
                ING SINKHOLE THAT SWALLOWED THE MUSTANG.

Online Model

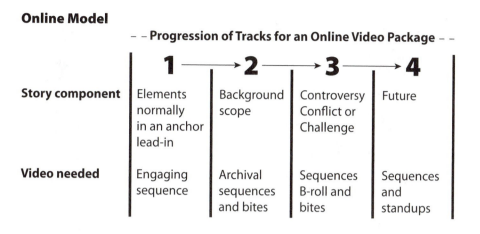

Figure 17.1 Diagram of a reporter's field package designed for Web-only distribution.

Track 1

County engineers are puzzled over the cause of the 25 foot deep . . .

But if the sinkhole story was slated for online only, the reporter would have to rewrite Track 1 and fold the studio lead-in into the first track. Here's what it might sound like:

Track 1

Hillsborough county engineers were out in force this morning . . . probing the depths of Tampa's newest attraction.

It's this 25-foot deep sinkhole behind the Mar Vista apartment complex . . . and it now contains resident Carly Heinz's Ford Mustang.

SOT Heinz   (It would be funny if I didn't need the car or had any way to get it out of the hole.)

Track 2 etc.

Internet tags to on-air stories. Clearly, this is the easiest addition to make. At the end of stories with extensive resources, the writer simply adds a sentence about the link to the station Web site. A CG adds emphasis to the referral. For some stations, this is mandatory for most stories.

Live o/c   A MAJOR NATIONAL RETAILER IS MAKING IT EASIER FOR ELECTIC CAR OWNERS TO TOP OFF THEIR CARS WHILE THEY SHOP.
THE BEST BUY CHAIN IS INSTALLING CHARGING STATIONS AT 12 OF ITS STORES IN ARIZONA . . . CALIFORNIA . . . AND WASHINGTON.

Figure 17.2 A live anchor broadcast during an ongoing sports parade is also on the Web site. When the over-the-air programming returns to regular shows, the live Internet coverage continues. Note the options placed to the right to suggest complimentary or alternative stories (courtesy KPIX).

	THE STATIONS ARE PART OF A PILOT PROGRAM CALLED THE E-V PROJECT . . . WHICH HOPES TO LOCATE 15-THOUSAND STATIONS IN THE FIRST YEAR ELECTRIC CARS ARE AVAILABLE.
CG lower 3rd	AND K-560'S WEB SITE AND FACEBOOK PAGE HAS A MAP SHOWING THE BEST BUY AND OTHER ELECTRIC VEHICLE CHARGING STATIONS IN OUR AREA.

Live feeds or raw field video from news conferences or events. This is simple enough. The video is linked to the site. It is popular for many audience members with plenty of time on their hands. (See Figure 17.2.)

Social Media

Social Media to Extend the Para-Social Relationships

As we mentioned in chapter one, social media sites such as Facebook or Twitter are invaluable in fostering relations with your audience. However, offhand remarks from the news staff can change this familiarity into a controversy. For this reason, it is vitally necessary to establish a written group or station policy about what can and cannot be said on these sites. All major networks have these policies.

News managers should mandate that reporters and on-air anchors assume all social media contributions are professional statements and that they should use the highest privacy tools. They warn against reposting company work, against revealing company material discussed in meetings, against violating other copyrights, and against joining forums that might suggest they support polarized political groups. But they also caution the news staff that anonymity granted to many on the Internet doesn't apply to newsgathering. In other words, the Internet doesn't change ethical standards.

Here's another suggestion posted in 2009 by National Public Radio:

Journalism should be conducted in the open, regardless of the platform. Just as you would do if you were working offline, you should identify yourself as an NPR journalist when you are working online. If you are acting as an NPR journalist, you must not use a pseudonym or misrepresent who you are. If you are acting in a personal capacity, you may use a screen name if that is allowed by the relevant forum.

You should always explain to anyone who provides you information online how you intend to use the information you are gathering.

However, the ultimate advice from NPR's posting was to consult with an editor if in doubt.

Social Media Gathers Feedback

Stations have found that social media reduces the audience's anxiety about contacting a news station with a news tip or criticism. Wise managers have designated staff members to answer every audience posting or tweet unless unless it is an obvious rant.

Social Media Solicits Citizen Journalist Submissions

Social media pages can be designed to stress the need for the audience to join in the newsgathering process, either by tweeting in tips, referring sites, or submitting photos and video. News departments, however, must be very careful to check out the volunteer material for authenticity.

Chapter Summary

Clearly, the ability to expand the news distribution, to pinpoint regional news to a more defined audience, and to build para-social relationships is a rapidly changing opportunity for traditional news agencies. Finding the right balance between staffing the on-air effort and the Web site is a continuing experiment for managers.

18

Ethical and Legal Accountability in the Web Age

Journalism doesn't happen a vacuum. What you write for the air or the Internet can defame someone in many ways. Reporters and writers need to study the ethical and legal boundaries for their work.

Although print and broadcast legal considerations have a long history in case law, the Internet's relationship to defamation and intellectual property cases is constantly changing and has left both writers and news subjects in a legal limbo.

Ethics, which studies decision making within a framework, also comes with controversy. Some make a case that actions should be judged relative to the goals of the individual case while others argue that every undertaking should be evaluated against a rigid code of standards.

Glossary

DEFENSE An element of the defendant's case in defamation law that either absolves or lessens the responsibility for libel/slander/invasion of privacy.

ETHICS The study of moral decision making in personal or social situations. Codes of ethics are frameworks and references for making decisions in news work.

FAIR USE An unlicensed but legal use of copyrighted material for insertion in news or commentary.

INVASION OF PRIVACY A form of defamation that, when broadcast, is true but injurious. Definitions of invasion of privacy vary from state to state.

LIBEL A form of injurious text or character defamation that, when broadcast, is false. The definitions of libel vary from jurisdiction to jurisdiction.

PRIVILEGED SITUATIONS In defamation law, any situations in which the court restricts libel charges because of the need for public knowledge. These situations include true and accurate reports of courts and lawmaking bodies.

SLANDER A form of defamation that is generally spoken and is injurious and false. Definitions of slander vary from state to state.

Ethics Involving News Work on Broadcast and Internet

What's it mean when we hear that journalists have low ethical standards? For many critics, it suggests that journalists will do anything—illegal, immoral, or whatever—to get a story. Journalists, they say, are only interested in building circulation or ratings. Are they right? I hope not.

Ethics is the study of decision making when that decision might lead to good or bad results. Ethical choices confront news staffs on a daily basis, whether about newsgathering methods, information release, production decisions, or story choice. In the past, there have been general agreements about which areas are ethically troublesome.

Ethics in the Internet Age

The opportunity to take a digital shortcut has increased with the Internet. In our current convergence world, journalists are faced with new questions that have no simple answers. For instance, should you pull something off Facebook and use it in a political race, even if the Facebook post was done by the opposing candidate? This situation faced a Reno, Nevada, station when a gubernatorial candidate was caught making off-message remarks during a speech. The opposition recorded it and pulled a damaging bite and posted it. The station ran the YouTube portion of the controversial statement but carefully made clear its source and explained in minute detail how they had attempted to get comment or feedback from the speaker in the YouTube video. This point-by-point description of the reporting process revealed the extensive effort they made to pursue the story and to anticipate any criticisms. I think they covered their bases for their obvious use of an opponent's attack video.

The Consequences of a News Story

Journalists are usually involved in two areas of consequences—personal and societal. In personal ethical decisions, the questions revolve around the protection of confidential sources, distortion of news items, outright lies, self-censorship, and conflict of interest in the selection of news items. In the societal professional area, there are issues of legal reporting, defamation and slander, checkbook journalism, cronyism with news sources, misrepresentation, invasion of privacy, stolen documents, and sensationalism.

That's a big list and a dangerous one. Journalists work in the community and use the public trust as a basis for their work. Because they seldom have legal standing beyond that of a private citizen, and because the first amendment questionably protects the news gathering area, reporters are often at odds with other rights and privileges. Even so-called shield laws, designed to protect unpublished notes and important sources, seldom stand up to the judicial challenges when pitted against the right to a fair trial.

Providing a checklist so journalists can test their decisions is a difficult task—there are just too many variables in each case study to claim it is a model. Instead, writers of ethics books have tried to set up general guidelines for decisions.

Louis Day, in his book *Ethics in Media Communications: Cases and Controversies*, listed six prioritized categories a journalist should consider when facing a particularly troubling situation. These are

1. Individual conscience (your own moral standards)

2. Objects of moral judgment (who is affected by your story)

3. Financial supporters (the company you work for)

4. The institution (journalism itself)

5. Professional colleagues (your coworkers)

6. Society (general taboos against certain actions)

As you can see, consideration begins with the individual's own moral conscience, then considers those immediately affected, before considering larger and more inclusive groups. In examining the situation in which a journalist is asked to reveal the identity of a confidential source, the decision process might go this way:

Define the problem. Be careful to consider all possible outcomes and individuals and groups affected. Here is an example:

Situation: A court is asking the journalist to reveal a source's name. The journalist has promised that source complete confidentiality. If the journalist refuses the court's request, the judge is ready to send the journalist to jail. Let's consider each possibility.

- Individual conscience: The journalist may decide that his or her own personal standards and values will be harmed. On the flip side, the jail option and ensuing court appearances may be damaging to a personal career and to the journalist's family.

- The objects of moral judgment: How does this affect the subjects of the story or the sources for information? Would releasing the source's name put this person in danger? Or cost the source his job? Would holding back the name injure a defendant's possibility for a fair trial? Is the name that important?

- Financial supporters: Yes, it is necessary to consider the effect on the employers. Court sanctions and fines have put news companies out of business and the continued fight against the judge's contempt power might cost the station thousands of dollars in fines and legal costs. Can the business stand the cost?

- The institution: Will this stand by the journalist be good or bad for credibility? Will the publicity damage the reputation of all who work for the station? Remember the national outrage over a network news producer's decision to use model rocket motors to assist the ignition of spilled gasoline in the crash-testing of a truck's fuel tank. A national poll by the Times Mirror Company found that the network's credibility had fallen significantly in the public's eye, and possibly management's concerns then coincided with the resignation of the division news president as well as the dismissal of several staff members who worked on the episode.

- Professional colleagues: You are asking if your coworkers would support your decisions. In this case, withholding the name of a confidential source, you might easily have them on your side because this has always been a journalist's badge of honor—not to reveal a source's name, even when threatened with jail.

- Society: This is the area of social responsibility. Journalists should believe that a society is stronger when a source can contact a reporter without fear of retribution and thus allow journalism to be in the watchdog role. It might be a tougher decision if the case involved broadcast of overly violent sensational video. In that case, societal reaction would figure more in the decision.

Your News Agency's Policies on Ethical Behavior

News departments or Web sites should have a clear, written policy about what is considered proper use of information and actuality when reporting or preparing news. It is often buried in a file drawer and no one has seen it. These policies might range from a general suggestion that all must be honest and truthful to very specific suggestions about the use of ambient audio versus imported wild sound.

Ethics of Reporting

When gathering information for a story, there will be many questions about what is proper and honest. These can be broken into several segments.

- Misrepresentation. In what cases can a journalist hide his or her identity to gather a story? Some say never. Some say it's possible if a greater societal injustice is being exposed.

- Lack of consent. Does a journalist always have to obtain consent to use news material? How much material from another publication may a journalist use before it violates Fair Use guidelines? Can a journalist make his or her own decisions about what is on or off the record? Can a journalist use legally confidential or sealed material, and if he or she does, who will go to jail for this? Often these questions get into the relative social value of the story.

- Getting involved. Should a reporter become part of the news story when someone needs help? Often the guidelines suggest this may happen if other resources are not available.

- Conflict of Interest-philosophy. Should a stated political position or contributions to a candidate disqualify a reporter from covering certain stories? This can be discussed endlessly.

- Conflict of Interest-financial. Should a reporter accept anything—including free admission to an event—if they are covering it? Some news stations have budgets that allow reporters to pay for everything, but smaller stations do not. A station I worked for had a policy that $25 was the cutoff limit for gifts to reporters. One holiday, a large screen television arrived at the newsroom addressed to the sports anchor. The obviously expensive item had a $24.99 price tag on it and was from a local professional sports team. He sent it back.

- Conflict of Interest-paying for news items. At times reporters are faced with a dilemma when a hard to get interviewee demands compensation for an exclusive interview. Whereas news stations in the United States vow they won't pay for news, there have been ways they have compensated demanding subjects.

Ethics of Writing Stories

Writers often are asked to translate another staff reporter's work into a coherent package for a newscast or Internet page. In these cases, there might be questions about interoffice politics when using a reporter's material.

- The attempt to get a response. Exactly how much effort must a writer undertake to contact a news subject for response? We discussed this in chapter 1. Must reporters make a maximum effort to reach obviously hostile spokespeople even if they expect no response? Absolutely.

Ethical Questions Using Video and Interviews

Whether shooting, editing, or writing against video, there are many situations that can be troublesome.

- Selectivity in using actualities. How much of an actuality must be used to indicate the context? Does an :05 soundbite represent the speaker's ideas?
    Not every interviewee is comfortable in front of a camera. May a reporter repeat questions to encourage an interviewee to make a broadcast-usable statement? How far can the reporter go in coaching an interviewee? Many say nothing should be done, whereas others say reporters can familiarize the interviewee with production methods.

- Sensational video. What is the station policy on use of sensational or violent video? Some producers suggest it draws attention to particularly difficult topics. Some argue that it is a part of life on the streets or in a war zone. There are suggestions it should not be broadcast at a certain time or placed on Web sites where children may see it.

- Staging video. Is it allowable to ask a subject to do something so it may be shot for your story? For instance, can you suggest they talk on the phone at their desk so you can shoot some cover? The discussion about this request for staging often revolves around how inconsequential the video is or whether the ambient sound from the staged video is important to the meaning of the story.

Ethical Questions Using Audio

Using audio might seem straightforward, but once again, there are opportunities for a shortcut and perhaps unethical approach.

- The use of music. Does a music bed underneath a story contribute to a different understanding of the material?

- Can a reporter doing an audio only story create sound effects if the real ones recorded on the scene have been lost?

- Should a reporter trim down the stumbling recorded answer of a favorite local personality to prevent embarrassment?

► **EXERCISE 18-A**

Ethical Analysis (group)

Read whichever situation you are assigned, then define the problem, and outline possible outcomes in any of the six areas of ethical consideration mentioned earlier. This can be done individually or in small groups.

- You are producer for a local television evening newscast. Your photographer returns to the station with video of a man who jumps from a third story window in a downtown hotel. Your news director thinks this is great actuality and should go in the newscast. What do you think? What must you take into account? Do you support or oppose using the video?

- You are a radio reporter who returns from a news conference called by a local critic of the city's police chief. In speaking about the latest controversial incident, the politician critic, who is obnoxious himself, becomes confused and actually issues a strong statement supporting the chief. You've been frustrated for a long time because this politician has been nasty to the media. Now he has hung himself out to dry. Your staff is eager to use it.

- You are a television reporter covering a highly publicized corruption trial in your city. One of the defense lawyers slips you some sealed grand jury transcripts with new information about the case. Although the judge has made a specific issue of forbidding any revelations from the transcripts during the trial, you believe that the information is in the public interest. What is your action and what might be the consequences?

- You are a reporter for a small radio station and a local gas and electric utility offers to fly you to the new hydroelectric plant for a visit. They will provide transportation, lodging, and meals for two days in an attractive resort area while you cover the details of the modern facility. Your low budget station could never pay for this. Do you take the story?

- While reporting a story about a highway accident, you and your cameraperson are asked by a nurse attending a severely injured person to transport him to the hospital. There is no other vehicle available. Your station, however, needs the story for the next newscast. Should you stop reporting and assume the role of a concerned citizen?

- Your public station has received a substantial amount of underwriting money from a laser hair removal clinic. Their spots, which are not called commercials, run before and after your newscast. Then you find you have been assigned to do a feature on laser hair removal, and the assignment desk has sent you to this same clinic to shoot the story. Should you do the story or complain?

- A criminal convicted in a sensational local case has never talked to the media. Now, she is calling you asking if you'd like to do an exclusive jailhouse interview. The catch— she wants $300 to help her child get an operation. Your station can afford this.

- Your reporter comes back with an interview of a very newsworthy person who has refused to talk to the media. You find out that your colleague, who identified himself as a reporter, wore a wireless mic and the photographer shot the interview from a parked van a half-block away. He obviously didn't tell the subject that she was being recorded. Should you use the video and sound? Does it matter whether or not this individual, who is involved in a public scandal, knows she was being recorded?

- A questionable Web site is touting a tabloid-like story about the indiscretions of a local celebrity. You like this entertainer and have always admired her performances. At the afternoon editorial meeting, you argue against using the story at all, contending that the Web site that is the source is trashy. Do you have a responsibility to investigate this story on your own?

Defamation

Libel, Slander, and Invasion of Privacy

Writers, reporters, and producers should be on the lookout for scripts that might injure someone with defamatory information. Although news staffers may not be versed in the finer points of libel, it is important to know when to start worrying about a phrase, a sentence, or an entire item. If the story looks questionable, consult the news manager or a company lawyer.

Defamation laws are state laws and differ across the country. (Ideally, the station should provide a summary of local statutes.) There are, however, some general concepts that apply throughout.

Three concerns in defamation are libel, slander, and invasion of privacy. Libel (and slander in many cases) is false information, is broadcast to an audience of more than one, clearly identifies a person, and injures the subject's reputation, relationships, or occupation. Usually, libel is written information; however, many states accept scripted broadcast material, even if it was spoken on the air, as libel. The consequences of libel can be quite severe, and libel judgments against small news agencies could put a radio or television station out of business.

Slander is basically the same as libel, except that it is spoken. In some states, it is considered to be impromptu speech and carries lesser weight in court.

Invasion of privacy involves a true story that identifies and harms. It covers the areas of private space intrusion, publication of private matters, putting a person in a false light, and the right to publicity. Generally, the categories concerning newswriters are the publication of private matters, most notably a criminal past, and using video to put a person in a false light. Federal courts have ruled that anything on the public record, such as arrests and court decisions, may be reported. You will run into trouble, however, when your story about someone's past includes material from unofficial sources. To defend against invasion of privacy, reporters have to prove the newsworthiness of the material.

The Internet is a different story in terms of libel. The question of who is responsible for libelous material is in flux and, in many cases, it is the writer who becomes the defendant. The question of responsibility varies from jurisdiction to jurisdiction and from country to country. Additionally, the spread of material in a viral sense is confusing and makes it hard to track what damage has been done. The source may be anonymous. The aggregator site with the material may be acting as a distributor rather than a publisher. The courts have yet to rule definitively on many questions.

Why Study Libel at All?

There are three good reasons. You could save someone's reputation by heading off a flawed and poorly researched story. This is worth the effort because reputations, even for people not immediately likeable, are hard to repair after they have been publicly trashed. An example was the media frenzy around Atlanta resident Richard Jewell in 1996, when it was thought he might be responsible for a public park bombing. Reporters followed him everywhere and he was seared with innuendo. Eventually cleared, he went on to sue several publications.

Second, and a bit on the defensive side, you can stay out of court and avoid litigation. This saves you time (going to court is tedious and may take months) and in the end may also save your job and even your employer.

Last is the aggressive reason. Know the libel laws and you'll know when you are in the right and can push a story or an investigation. Threats of libel suits may send you to the lawyers, but they won't automatically stifle the controversial stories.

For Libel to Exist

Certain general conditions have to exist for libel to occur:

- *Identification.* Even if accidental, a verbal or visual identification of a person to the satisfaction of the listeners or viewers is sufficient for the courts. This can also happen if you identify a person as a member of a small, exclusive group; however, in that case, the others in that group may sue too.

    Be cautious when working with visuals. A close-up of someone's face on the air while your copy talks about drugs, offensive illnesses, and so on, is enough to set off a libel suit—as long as the identification is solid.

- *Dissemination.* The message has to be distributed to at least one person and in any form. A news agency can be sued even if the material does not appear over the air, in print, or on the Internet.

- *Injurious.* This is what it's all about. Your story could injure (1) a person's reputation, (2) his or her ability to have friends, or (3) a profession. The false statement must be something of verifiable fact and not an offhand opinion. In the same fashion, you can libel a corporation and injure its ability to do business.

- *False.* Libel is false. If the story is true, there is no libel.

Negligence or Malice

This is one of those odd twists. Quite likely, if the mistake gets on the air or Internet, you will already have been negligent. Negligence, however, is different from malice. If you are simply negligent, the damage award might be small. But if the plaintiff proves malice, big money could change hands.

In a sense, **malice** is serious negligence and often involves the intent of the writer. If the plaintiff can prove the reporter planned to harm the individual in the story, no matter what the truth, then it is an ironclad case. However, it is more likely that a second definition of malice will be involved and that means the reporter did not apply normal news-gathering safeguards and practices to this story. This could suggest failing to consult multiple sources, ignoring research, or whatever. This type of malice is generally proven by testimony that you just didn't make an all-out journalistic effort to find out whether your information was true or not.

If malice is proven, private persons who have already proven libel can ask for additional multimillion-dollar punitive damages. Even more in damages can be at stake if public persons can sue you for libel about stories involving their public duties.

How Do You Distinguish a Private Person From a Public Person?

Courts have decided there are two general classes of injured parties who may sue for libel. There are those who have remained out of the public eye, carrying on their lives without seeking public office or publicity. These are private people. The majority of the people you interact with when gathering news are private citizens. When false and damaging information is broadcast about private persons, they are likely to collect damages.

But so-called public persons are viewed with a different standard. The courts have ruled there must be some leeway for news reporters who constantly work with information about persons who voluntarily or involuntarily ended up in the public eye. Sometimes stories, although based on proven sources, will be wrong. Therefore, less stringent standards are applied when public persons sue for libel. Even if the story is not true, public persons must prove actual malice was involved.

The line separating a public and private person is ill defined. The courts have gone back and forth over the years, and there is no set legal definition. Usually, if a person voluntarily inserts himself or herself into the public eye (for example, if a candidate runs for office or a massive amount of publicity is put out about some entertainment star), that person can be considered a public person.

Someone can also involuntarily move into the public arena by becoming involved in an unexpected but highly public event. The court ruled that Oliver Sipple, the bystander who slapped the gun hand of a suspect shooting at then-President Gerald Ford, had become a limited public person for a short time, and that the normal investigations into elements of his private life were acceptable pursuits of journalism. An invasion of privacy suit by Sipple was thrown out for that reason.

On the other hand, just because someone works for a municipality doesn't make him or her a public person under the law. The public person must be involved in controversial cases and must have access to the public to respond. Is a street cop a public person? Not necessarily so.

How About Consent?

What if the person agreed to an interview, then libeled 15 individuals in the answers to your questions? If the interview is cut into a story and goes out on the newscast, who is the responsible party? Who is going to get sued?

Anything you broadcast or put on the Internet is your responsibility. If you include a libelous statement in a story, and leave it as the sole reference without any other sources or perspective, then you and your news agency might be heading to court. Because someone says something in an interview doesn't mean that it is legal or truthful. You have the right to use that quote but also the responsibility to report on its accuracy.

Privileged Situations

"Privilege" here refers to a "fair and true report" of the community's official business. In many jurisdictions, if you are reporting the actions of any official court proceeding, or publicly assembled federal, state, or municipal government body, you are a surrogate for the public and may report what went on, even if what happened was libelous. Therefore if one lawmaker referred to the other in a false and damaging way, you may report it, as long as it is an accurate account.

A caution: This "privilege" does not apply to statements outside the courtroom, the legislative chambers, or the city council meeting room. Even if you give a fair and accurate account of a news conference in the hallway after the event, the shield of privilege is gone.

Statute of Limitations

Many jurisdictions have a set time that the libel/slander must be contested. In California, it is a year from the date of the libel and then one year from each subsequent publication or broadcast of the material. So, if you get into defamation trouble, don't rebroadcast the story.

Defenses

Once a court or jury determines libel has occurred, the journalist may present defenses to mitigate damage awards. The best, of course, is truth. But others, including usually reliable sources, deadline pressure, or strict adherence to journalistic standards, may prevent the court from imposing punitive damages, which would cost you the most.

Still Worried?

It is often impossible for reporters, untrained in the law, to be up-to-date on all defamation laws. When a question arises, check with the executive producer, the news director, or the station attorneys. Be prepared to back up your angle with facts, multisource research, and knowledge of the law. Otherwise you may get an overcautious decision from these people, who know all too well what a libel suit can do to the station.

▶ **EXERCISE 18-B**

Libel

Examine this story for libel. Circle any possible problems open for discussion.

O/C   THE BLUE BEACH BOARD OF EDUCATION TODAY REMOVED AN ELEMENTARY SCHOOL PRINCIPAL FOR CHARGES OF CHILD ABUSE.

BOARD OFFICIALS WOULDN'T REVEAL THE NAME OF THE PRINCIPAL . . . SAYING ONLY THAT SHE WORKED IN ONE OF FOUR PINE DISTRICT SCHOOLS.

THE BOARD STATEMENT SAYS PARENTS HAD CHARGED THE PRINCIPAL WITH IMPROPERLY TOUCHING CHILDREN AFTER SCHOOL HOURS IN HER OFFICE.

TWO WEEKS AGO . . . IRATE PARENTS AT MILLDOWN SCHOOL INTERRUPTED A BOARD MEETING TO COMPLAIN ABOUT PRINCIPAL LOUISE GITTLER.

THE DISTRICT ATTORNEY'S OFFICE HAS NOT FILED CHARGES.

▶ **EXERCISE 18-C**

Libel 2

Given the information about damaging statements in this chapter, examine this entertainment story for libel. Circle any possible problems.

THE LEAD SINGER OF THE MUSIC GROUP THE WANTON TWITS IS SAYING THE BAND WON'T APPEAR IN THE MARCH THIRD BIG STEEL CONCERT,

LEICESTER AREA FANS HAVE ALREADY BOUGHT NINE-THOUSAND TICKETS TO THE TWITS CONCERT . . . SOMETIMES PAYING AS MUCH AS 135-DOLLARS PER TICKET.

TWITS MANAGER AND SINGER AAZY PERCH SAYS THEY DON'T WANT TO WORK WITH PROMOTER LYLE LEFEVER. PERCH SAID LEFEVER WAS A TWO-FACED LIAR WHO STOLE MONEY FROM THEM . . . AND DRUGGED THEM WITH DOCTORED REFRESHMENTS SET ON THE TABLE DURING CONTRACT TALKS.

LEFEVER WAS NOT AVAILABLE FOR COMMENT.

> **EXERCISE 18-D**

Invasion of Privacy

Examine this story for invasion of privacy. Discuss in class what you think are areas of concern.

O/C   A MAN WHO WANTS TO BE THE NEW BUSINESS MANAGER OF ROWART COUNTY HAS A LONG CRIMINAL RECORD.
RICHARD STERN ADMITTED THE CHARGES THIS AFTERNOON.
NEWSPAPER ACCOUNTS SAY THE ARRESTS ALL HAPPENED MORE THAN 10 YEARS AGO AND INVOLVED BAD CHECKS AND CREDIT CARDS.
STERN SAYS NONE OF THE ARRESTS HAD GONE TO COURT AND SOLUTIONS HAD BEEN WORKED OUT WITH THE BANKS. HE ADMITTED THAT IT HAPPENED AT A TIME IN HIS LIFE THAT HE WAS . . . QUOTE . . . GOING THROUGH A ROUGH PATCH.
ANOTHER CANDIDATE FOR THE JOB MADE THE CHARGES PUBLIC.

Intellectual Property, Copyright, and Fair Use

This workbook is not going to summarize these legal situations. It's a complex area best investigated on primary legal sites. In traditional broadcast or print, the ability of reporters or commentators to use unlicensed copyrighted material is clearly defined in some cases and vague in others.

For the Internet, the question becomes fuzzier. Reporters should be familiar with the boundaries of the Fair Use policy, and anyone editing video should understand questions of incidental use of copyrighted pictures and music.

Fair Use in Journalism or Commentary

The principle of fair use of copyrighted material cuts both ways for journalists and bloggers. Because they are allowed to take small portions of copyrighted works and use them in commentary, the large search engines may re-post the guts of stories for use in almost any site. But social media has made an enormous amount of private material available on accessible pages. The originator of this material might not be the person at the center of the controversy, but if it appears for general viewing on a site, it goes beyond the expectation of privacy. Using photos and material from these sources should be discussed with news managers.

Chapter Summary

It is useful for journalists to consider the effects of their stories and to take great care in any material that goes out on the air or online. There may be ethical problems in the material's acquisition and writing, and there may be expensive legal consequences of the broadcast.

INDEX